EASY PIANO

Torch Songs
A COLLECTION OF SULTRY JAZZ AND BIG BAND STANDARDS

D1484710

CONTENTS

ISBN 0-7935-8003-X

HAL•LEONARD®
CORPORATION

7777 W. BLUEMOUND RD. P.O. BOX 13819 MILWAUKEE, WI 53213

Visit Hal Leonard Online at
www.halleonard.com

AS LONG AS HE NEEDS ME

from the Columbia Pictures - Romulus film OLIVER!

Words and Music by
LIONEL BART

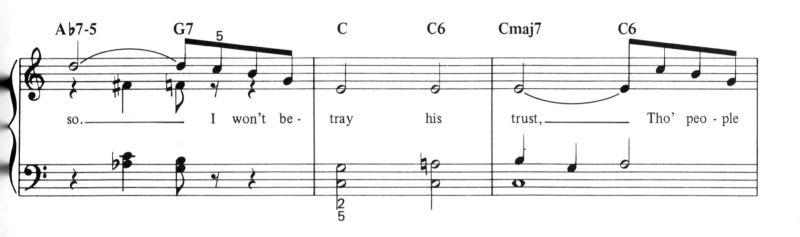

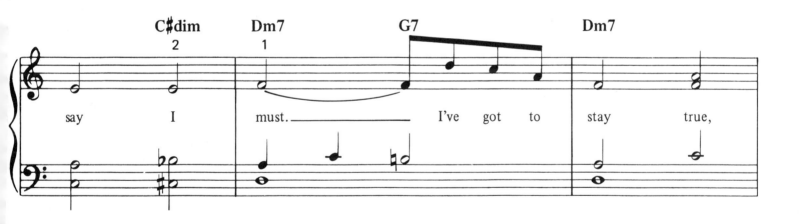

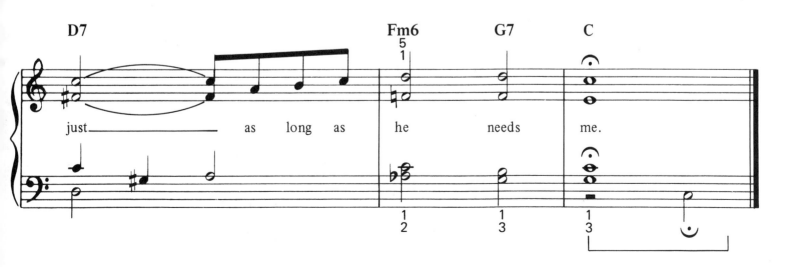

BEWITCHED
from PAL JOEY

Words by LORENZ HART
Music by RICHARD RODGERS

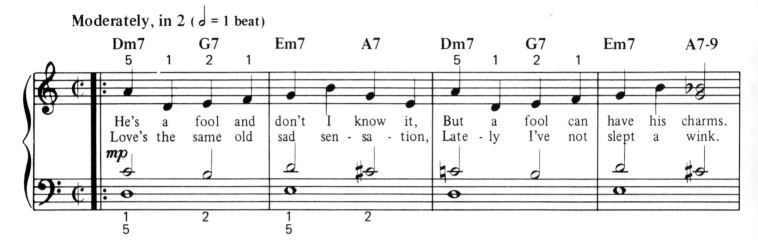

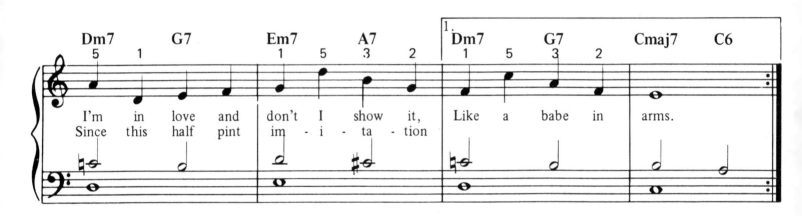

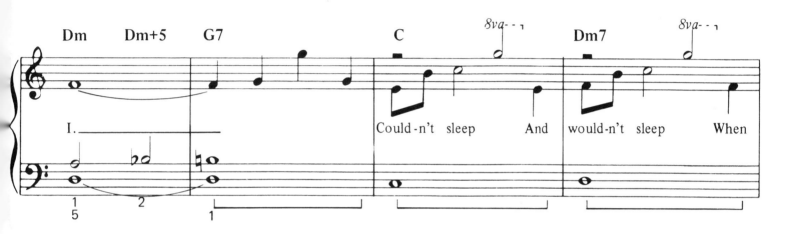

6

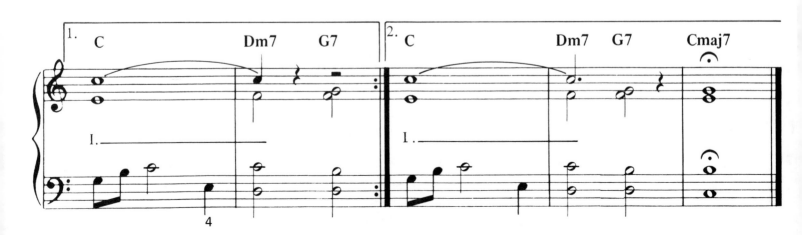

BLAME IT ON MY YOUTH

Words by EDWARD HEYMAN
Music by OSCAR LEVANT

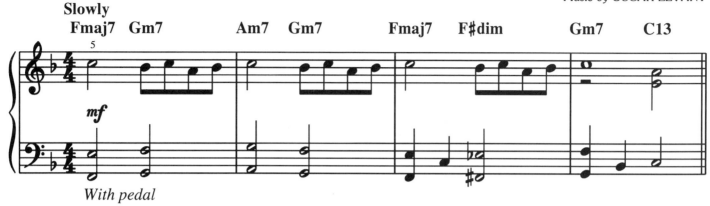

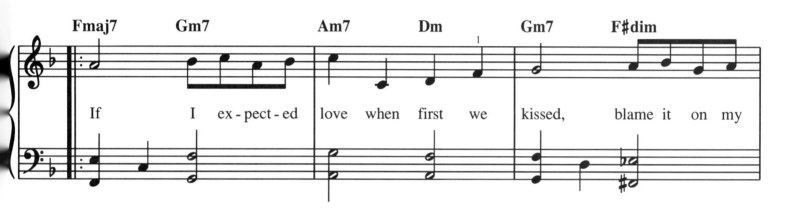

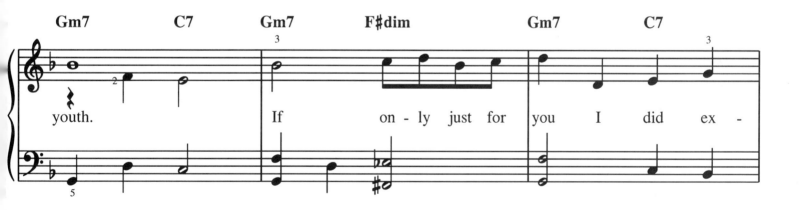

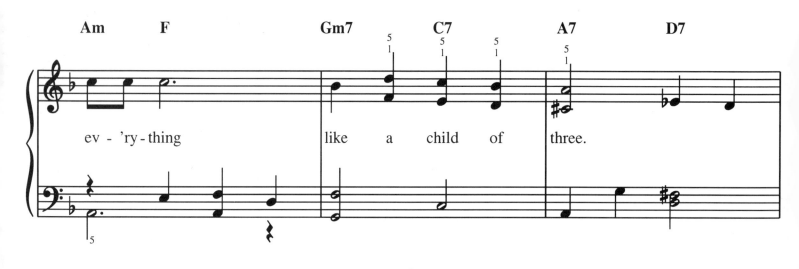

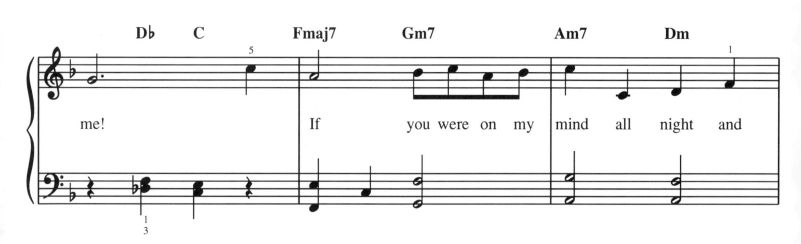

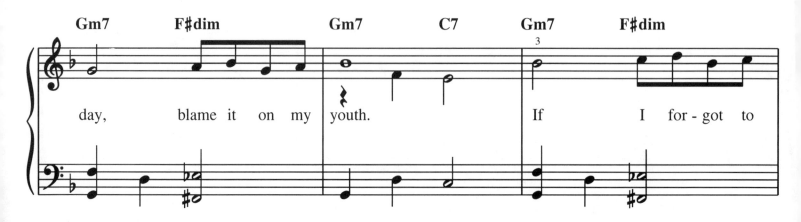

CAN'T HELP LOVIN' DAT MAN
from SHOW BOAT

Lyrics by OSCAR HAMMERSTEIN II
Music by JEROME KERN

COME RAIN OR COME SHINE

from ST. LOUIS WOMAN

Words by JOHNNY MERCER
Music by HAROLD ARLEN

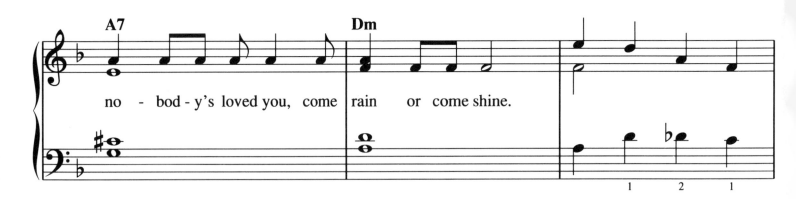

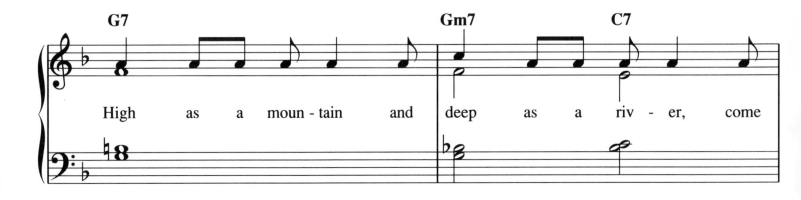

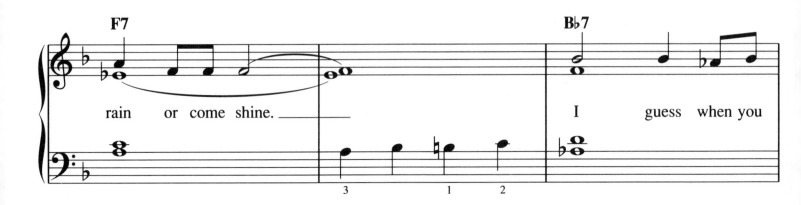

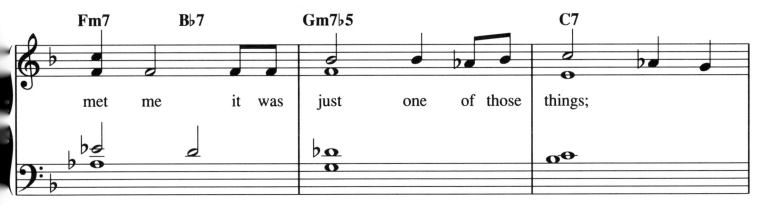

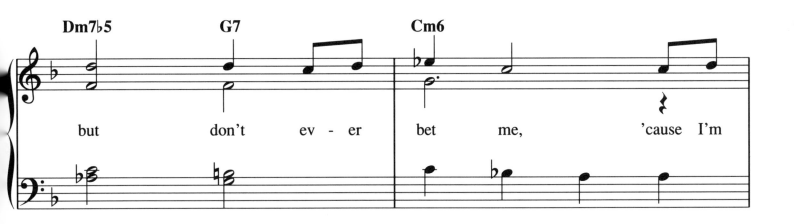

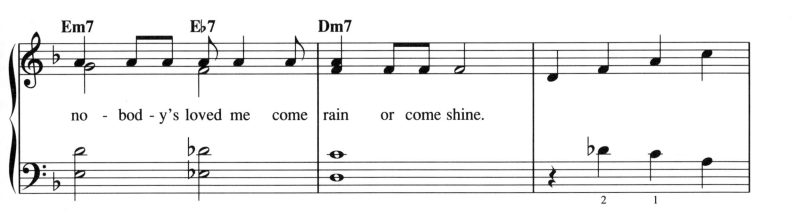

Hap - py to - geth - er, un - hap - py to - geth-er and won't it be fine.___

___ Days may-be cloud - y or sun - ny, we're

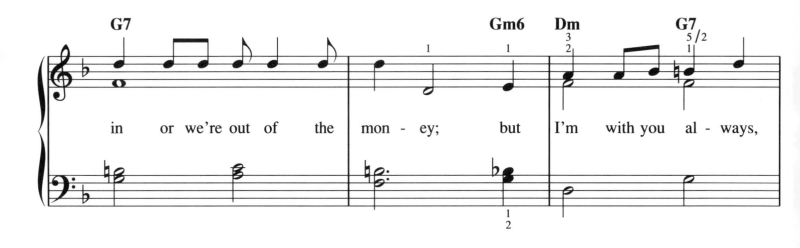

in or we're out of the mon - ey; but I'm with you al - ways,

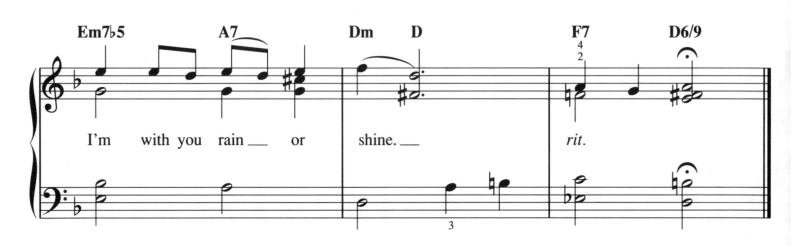

I'm with you rain ___ or shine. ___ *rit.*

CRY ME A RIVER

Words and Music by
ARTHUR HAMILTON

18

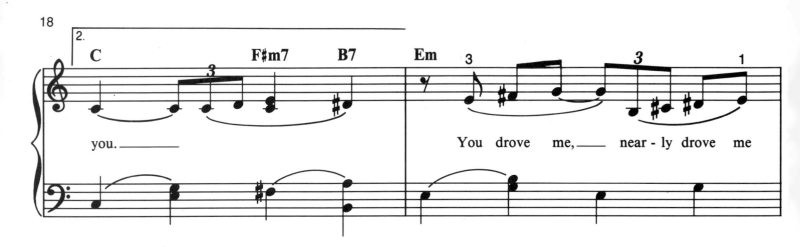

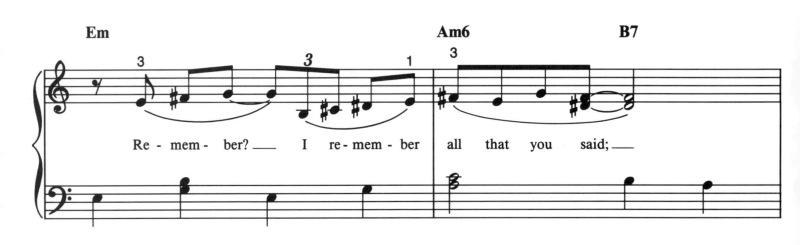

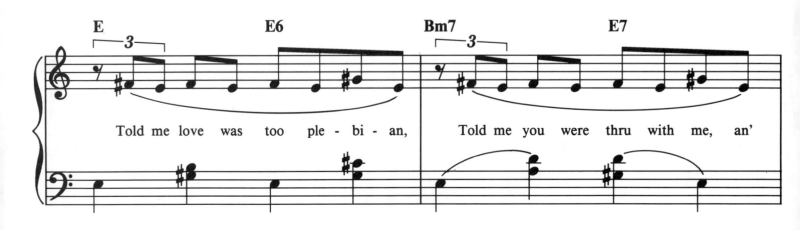

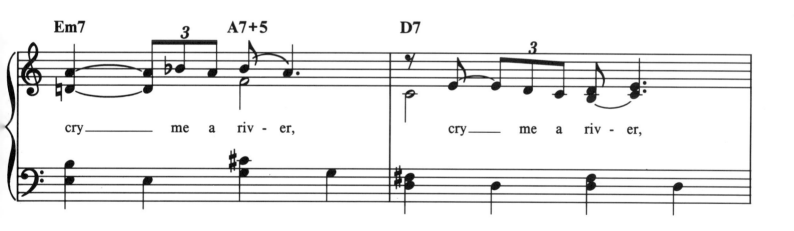

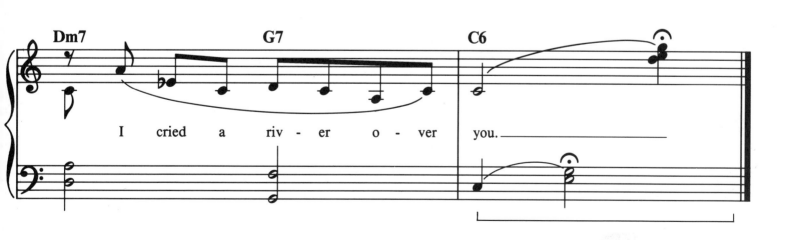

DO NOTHIN' TILL YOU HEAR FROM ME

Words and Music by BOB RUSSELL
and DUKE ELLINGTON

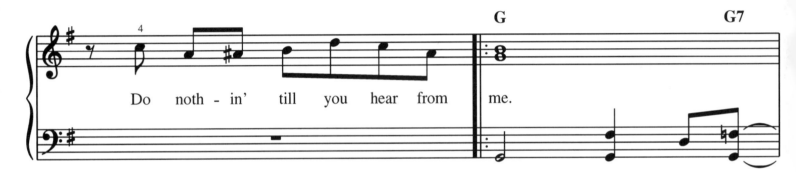

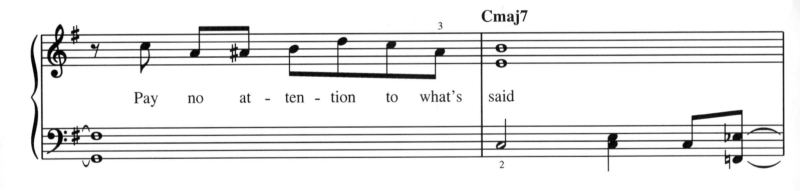

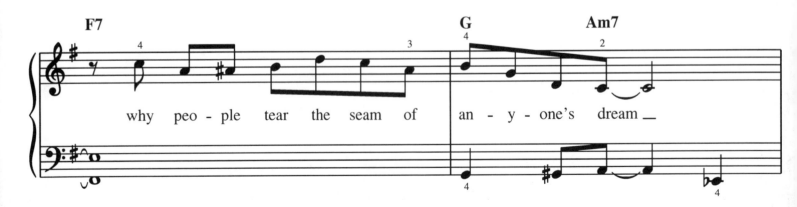

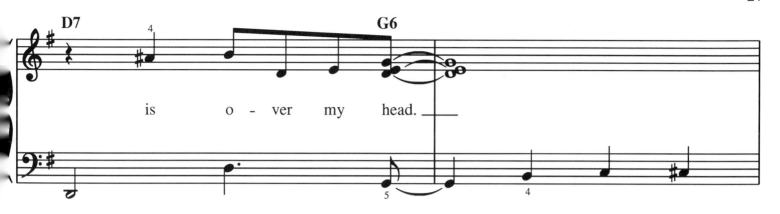

is o - ver my head. ___

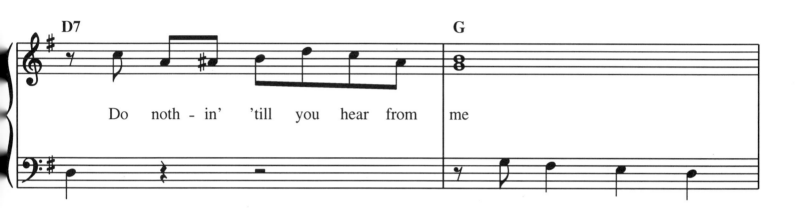

Do noth - in' 'till you hear from me

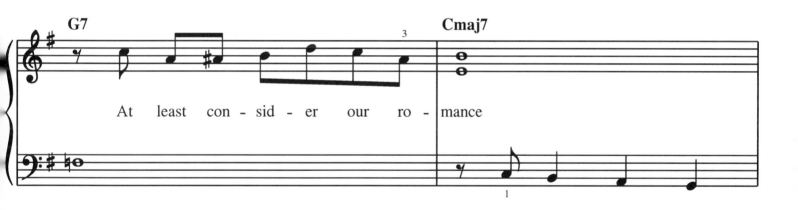

At least con - sid - er our ro - mance

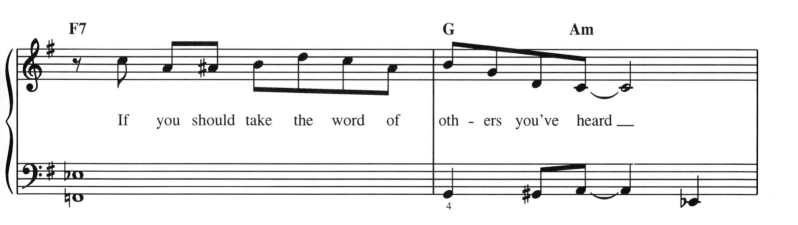

If you should take the word of oth - ers you've heard ___

22

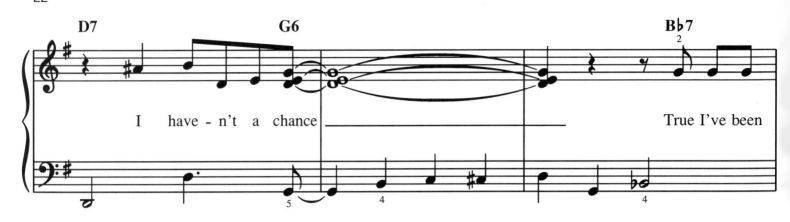

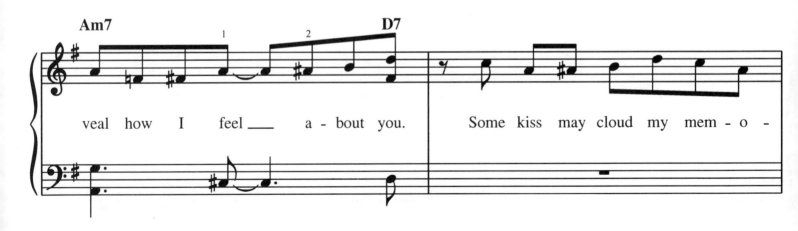

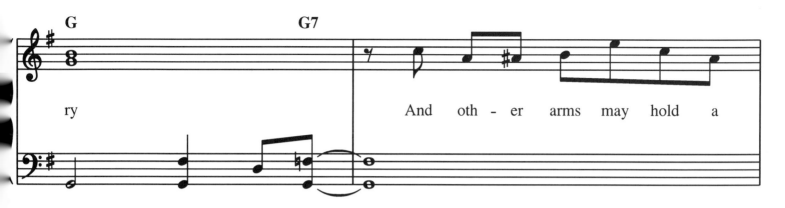

ry

And oth-er arms may hold a

thrill

But please do noth-in' till you

hear it from me ___

And you nev-er will. ___

Do noth-in' till you hear from ___

GET OUT OF TOWN

from LEAVE IT TO ME

Words and Music by
COLE PORTER

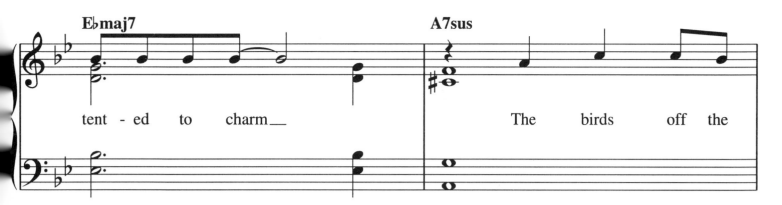

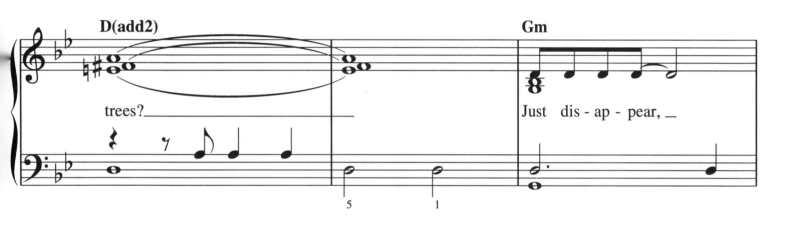

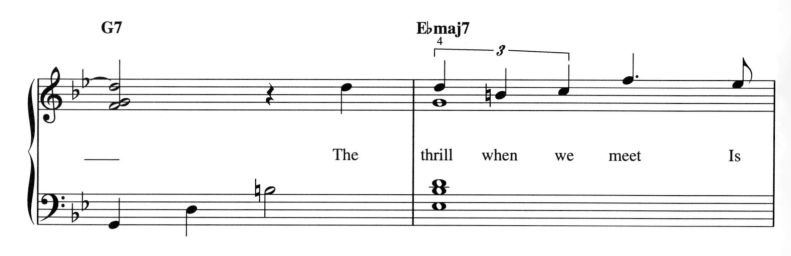

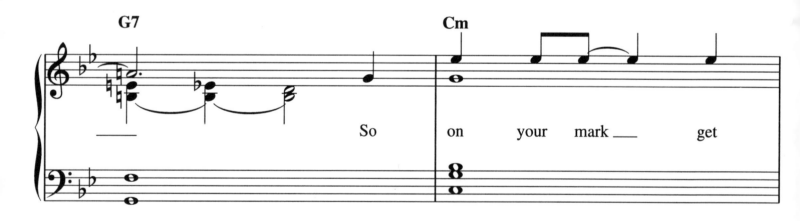

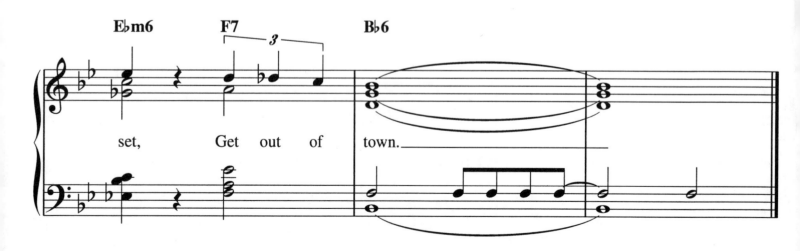

GLAD TO BE UNHAPPY

from ON YOUR TOES

Words by LORENZ HART
Music by RICHARD RODGERS

Fools rush in, so here I am

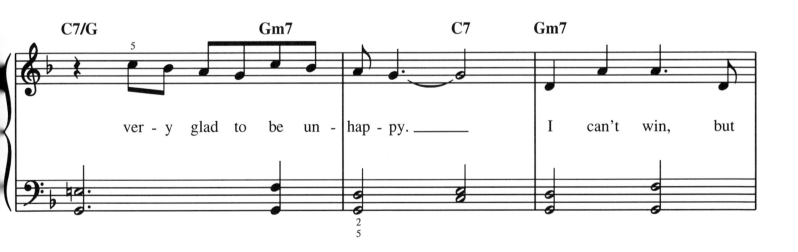

ver - y glad to be un - hap - py. _____ I can't win, but

28

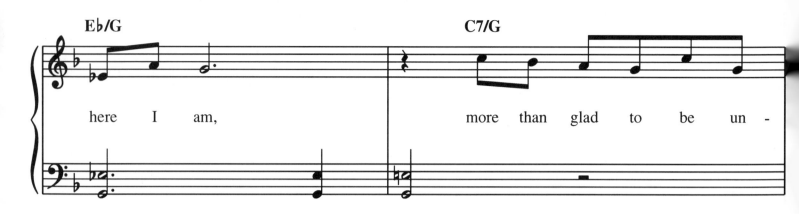

here I am,   more than glad to be un -

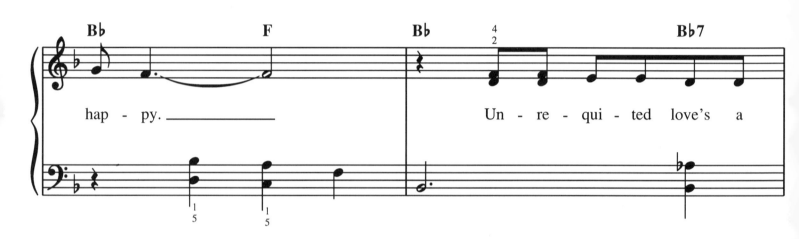

hap - py. _____   Un - re - qui - ted love's a

bore.   And I've got it pret - ty   bad,

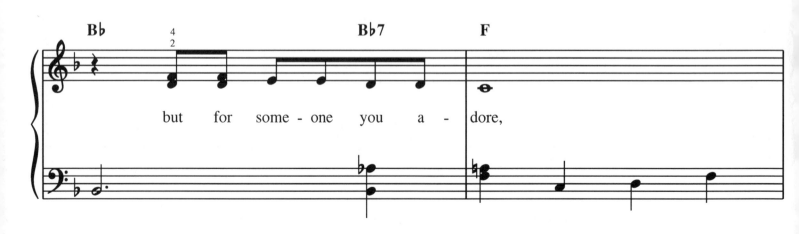

but   for   some - one   you   a - dore,

A GOOD MAN IS HARD TO FIND

Words and Music by
EDDIE GREEN

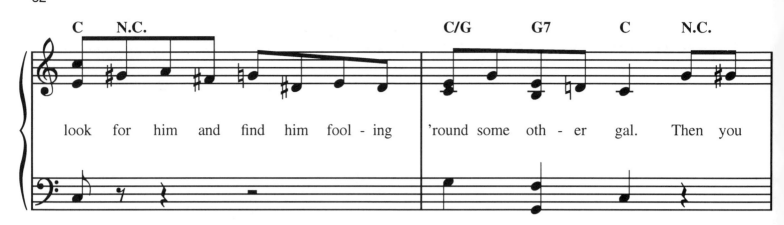

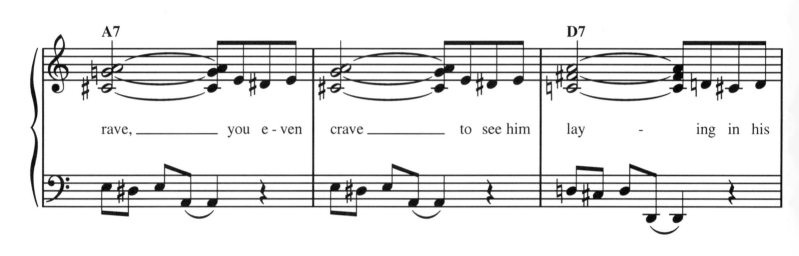

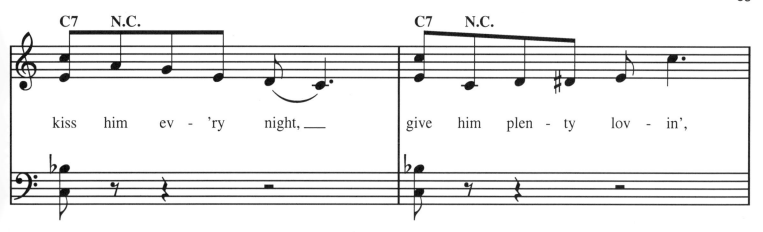

kiss him ev - 'ry night, ___ give him plen - ty lov - in',

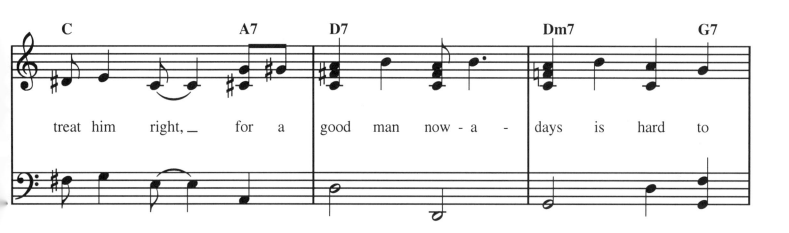

treat him right, _ for a good man now - a - days is hard to

1.

find. A good

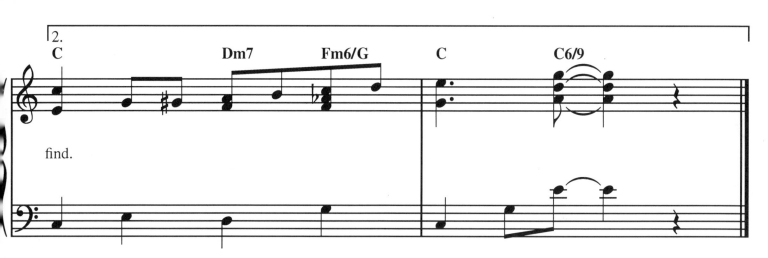

2.

find.

HERE'S THAT RAINY DAY
from CARNIVAL IN FLANDERS

Words by JOHNNY BURKE
Music by JIMMY VAN HEUSEN

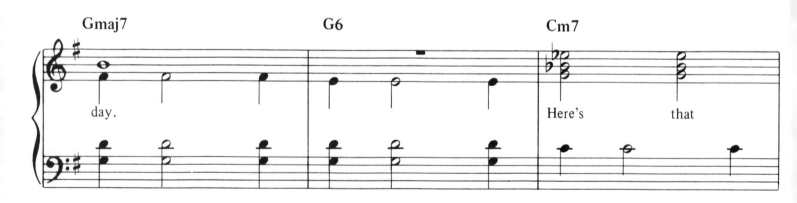

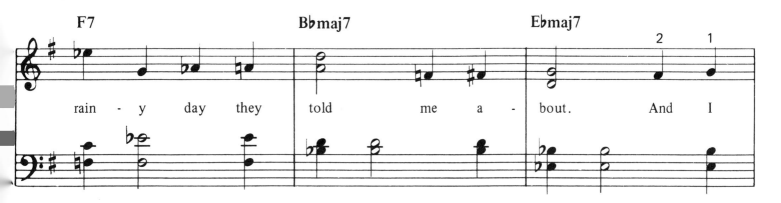

F7   B♭maj7   E♭maj7

rain - y day they told me a - bout. And I

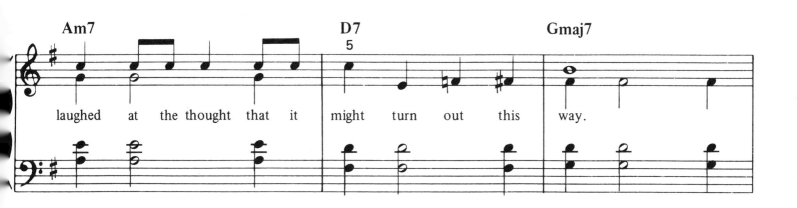

Am7   D7   Gmaj7

laughed at the thought that it might turn out this way.

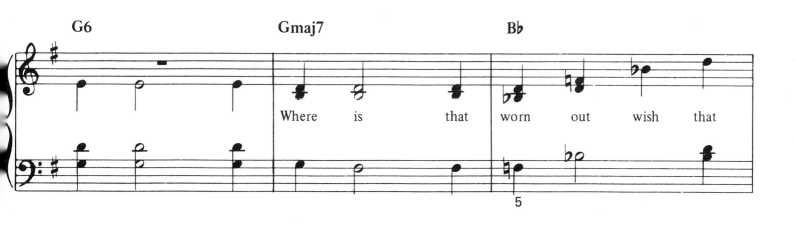

G6   Gmaj7   B♭

Where is that worn out wish that

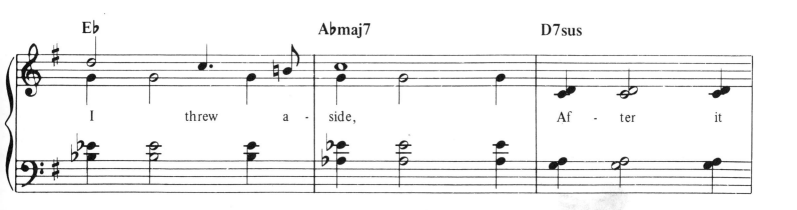

E♭   A♭maj7   D7sus

I threw a - side, Af - ter it

36

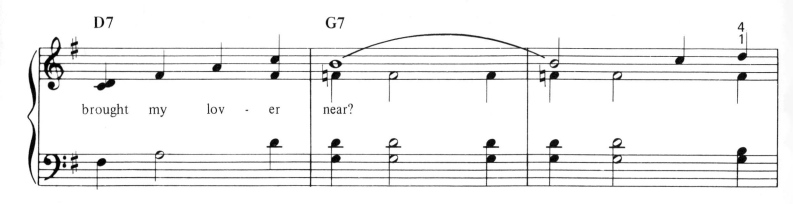

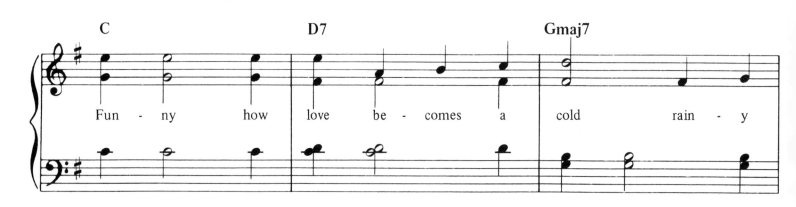

IF HE WALKED INTO MY LIFE

from MAME

Music and Lyric by
JERRY HERMAN

38

I CAN'T GET STARTED WITH YOU
from ZIEGFELD FOLLIES

Words by IRA GERSHWIN
Music by VERNON DUKE

42

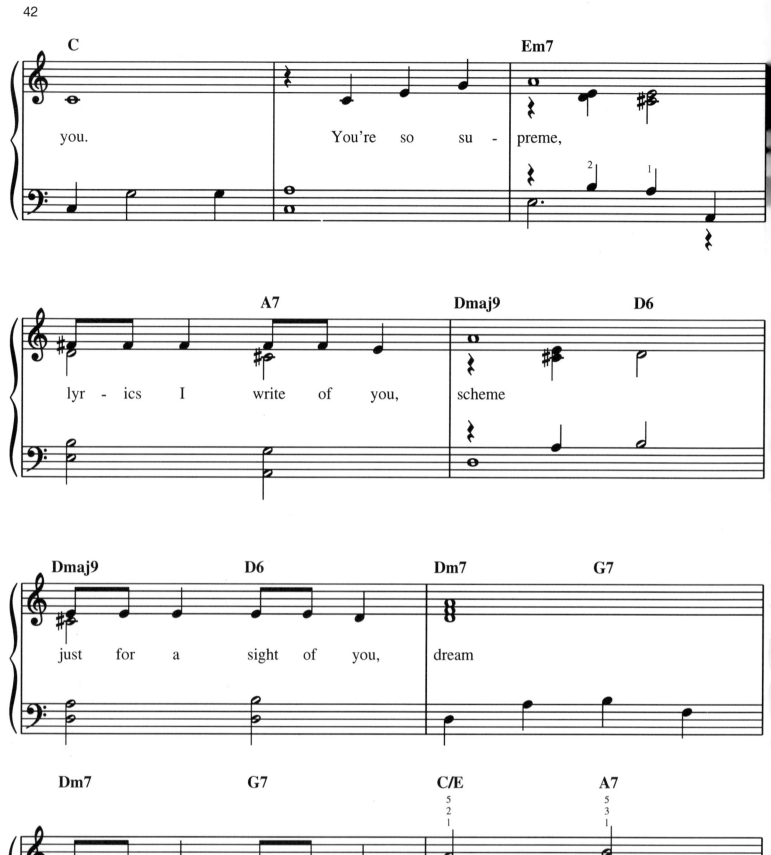

LOSING MY MIND
from FOLLIES

Words and Music by
STEPHEN SONDHEIM

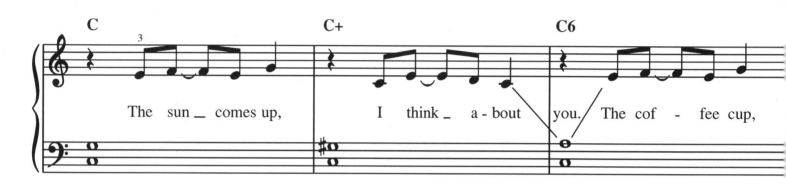

The sun _ comes up, I think _ a-bout you. The cof - fee cup,

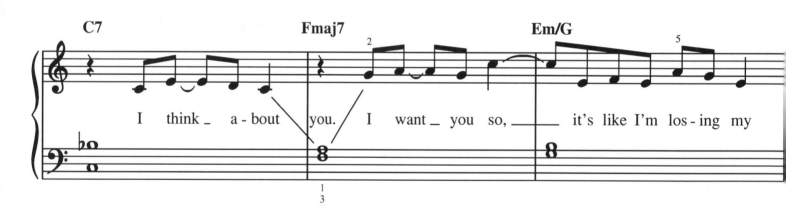

I think _ a-bout you. / I want _ you so, ____ it's like I'm los-ing my

mind. The morn - ing finds,

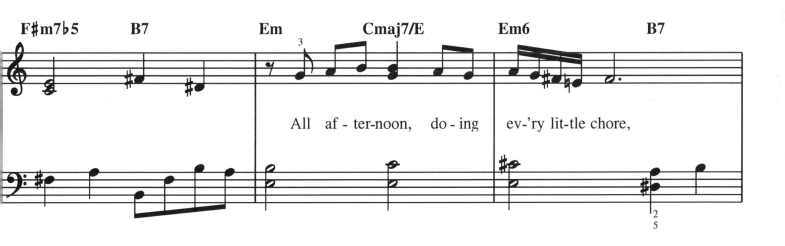

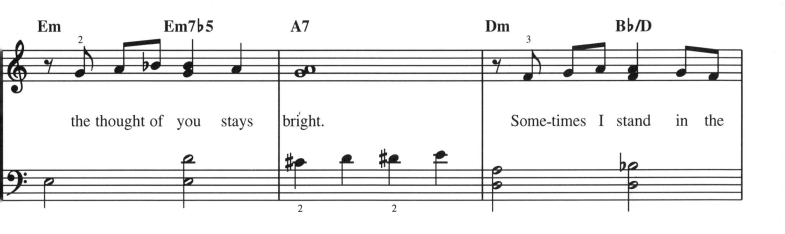

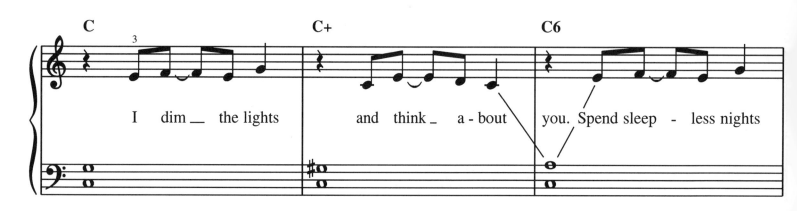

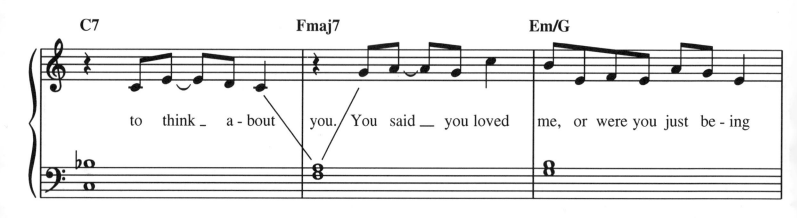

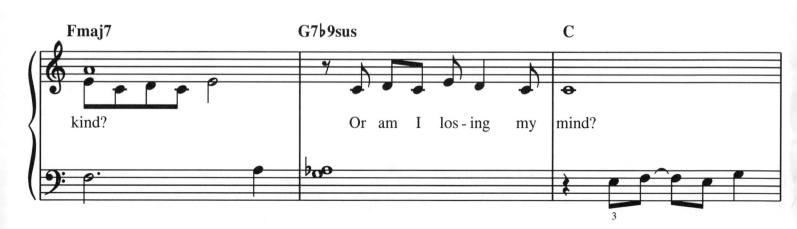

48

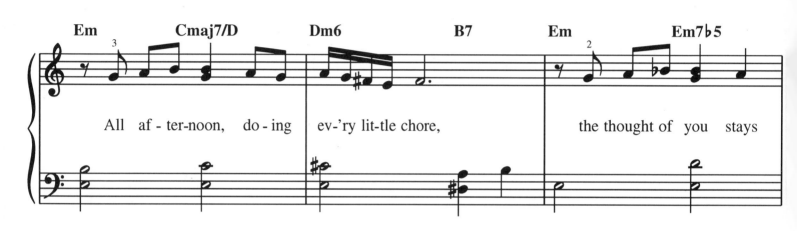

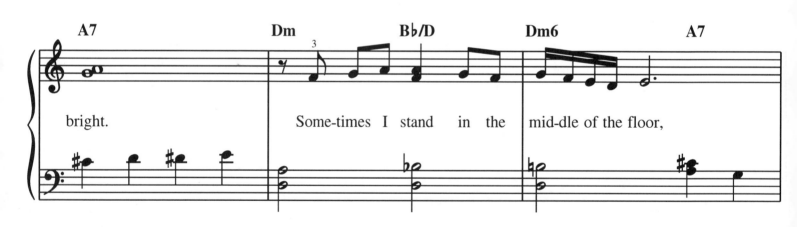

49

and think _ a-bout you, spend sleep - less nights, to think _ a-bout

you. You said _ you loved me _____ or were you just be-ing kind?

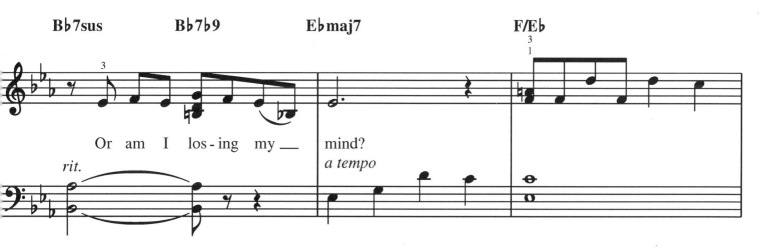

Or am I los-ing my _ mind?

rit.

a tempo

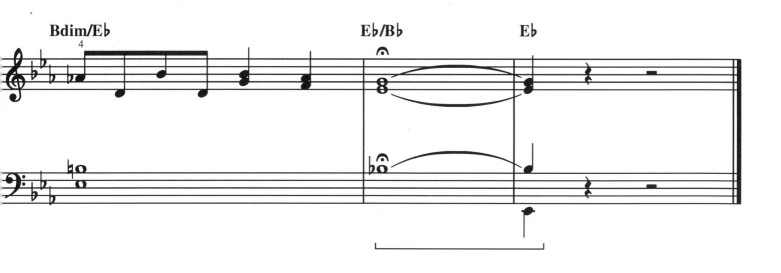

LOVE ME OR LEAVE ME

Lyrics by GUS KAHN
Music by WALTER DONALDSON

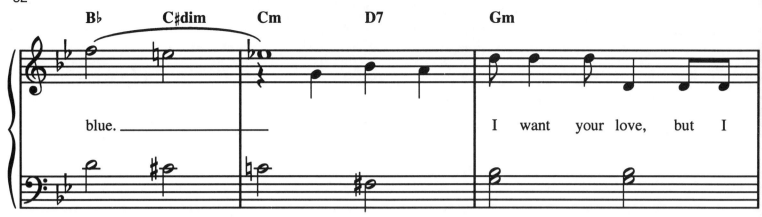

blue. _____

I want your love, but I

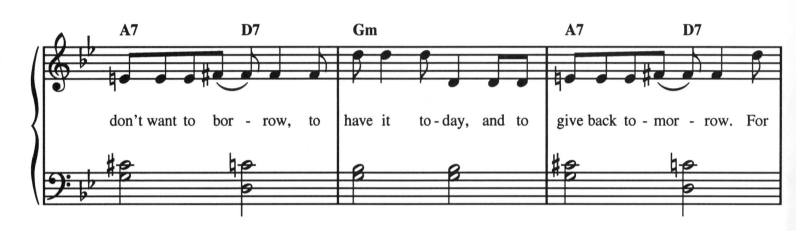

don't want to bor - row, to have it to - day, and to give back to - mor - row. For

my love is your love, there's no love for no - bod - y else!

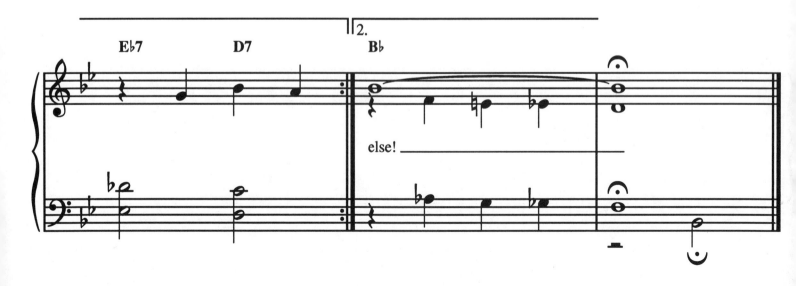

else! _____

MOOD INDIGO

from SOPHISTICATED LADIES

Words and Music by DUKE ELLINGTON,
IRVING MILLS and ALBANY BIGARD

54

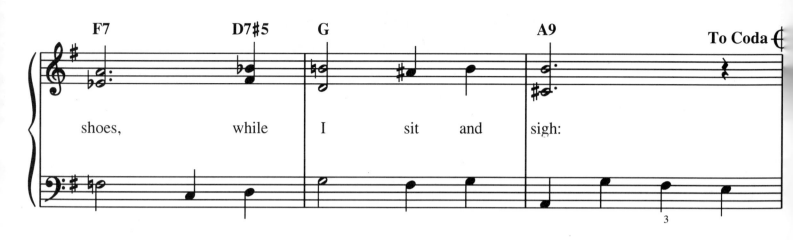

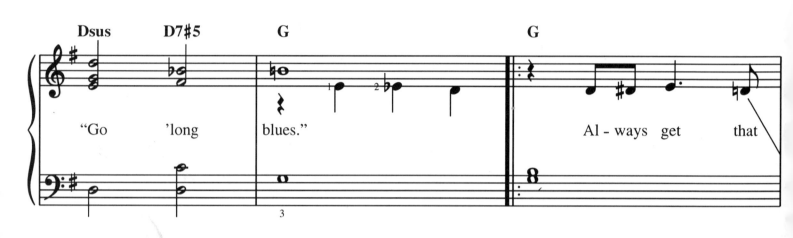

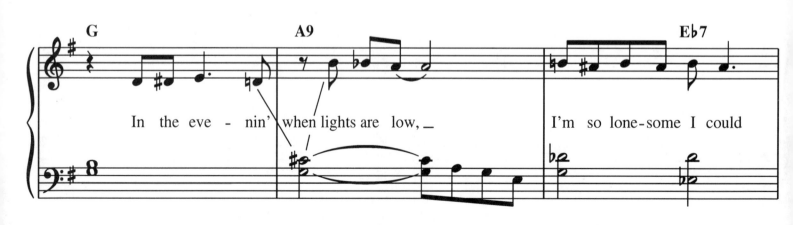

LOVER MAN
(Oh, Where Can You Be?)

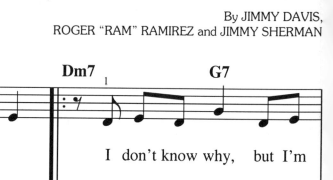

By JIMMY DAVIS,
ROGER "RAM" RAMIREZ and JIMMY SHERMAN

Slowly

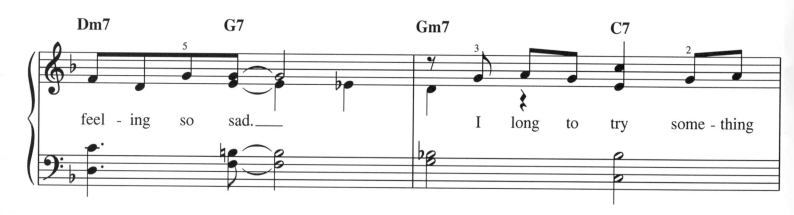

With Pedal

I don't know why, but I'm feel - ing so sad.___ I long to try some - thing

I've nev - er had,___ Nev - er had no kiss - in'

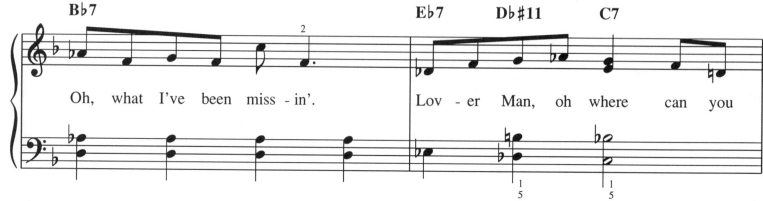

Oh, what I've been miss - in'. Lov - er Man, oh where can you

Thomas Chace
Piano Instruction/Live Entertainment
35 Hawthorne Ave.
Cranston RI 02910

Nov. 4, 2005   3 hours live music for Rhode Island Country Club member
dining room. $125.00

Nov. 11, 2005   3 hours live music for Rhode Island Country Club member
dining room. $125.00

Total Due as of 10/29/05 $250.00

Thank you for your business.

Thomas A. Chace

58

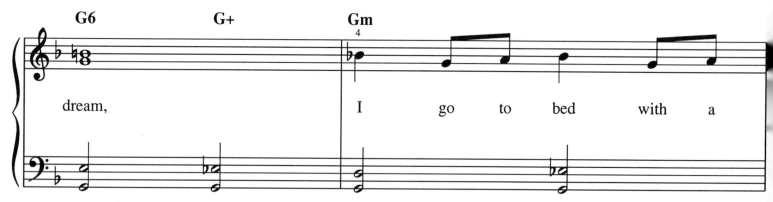

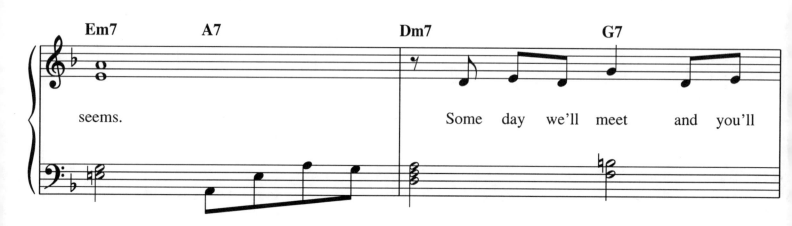

THE MAN THAT GOT AWAY

from the Motion Picture A STAR IS BORN

Lyric by IRA GERSHWIN
Music by HAROLD ARLEN

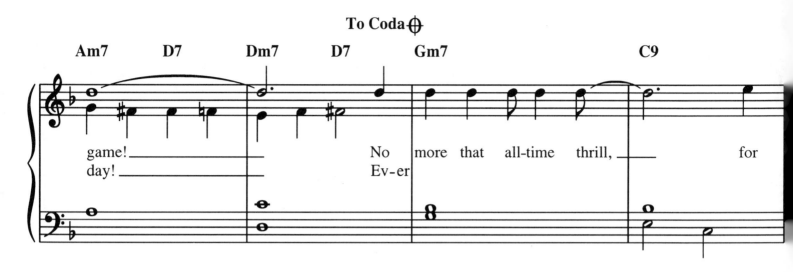

To Coda ✛

Am7　　　D7　　　Dm7　　　D7　　　Gm7　　　　　　C9

game! _____
day! _____　No more that all-time thrill, ___ for
　　　　　　　　　　Ev-er

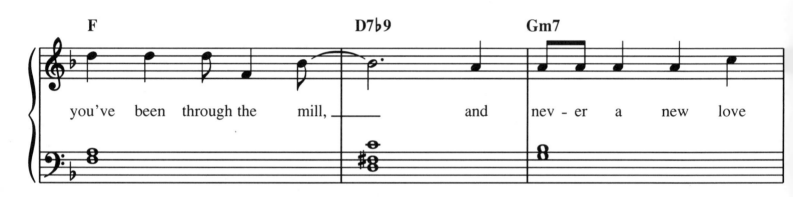

F　　　　　　　　　　　D7♭9　　　Gm7

you've been through the mill, ___ and nev-er a new love

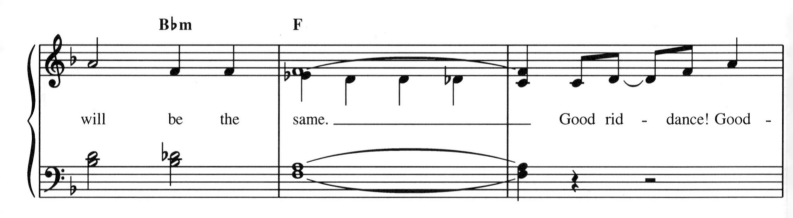

B♭m　　　F

will be the same. _____ Good rid - dance! Good -

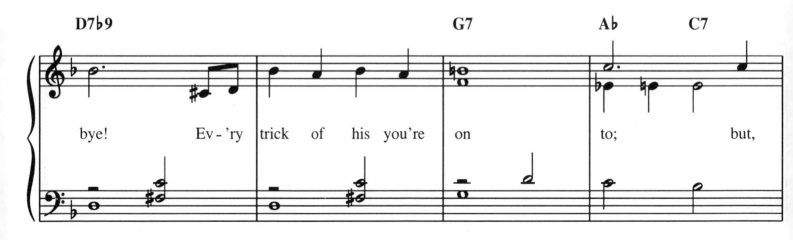

D7♭9　　　　　　　　G7　　　A♭　　C7

bye! Ev-'ry trick of his you're on to; but,

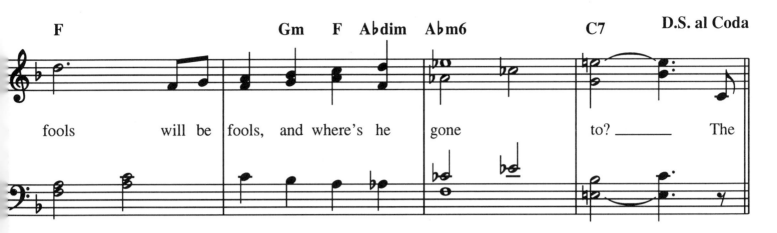

fools   will be fools, and where's he   gone   to? _____ The

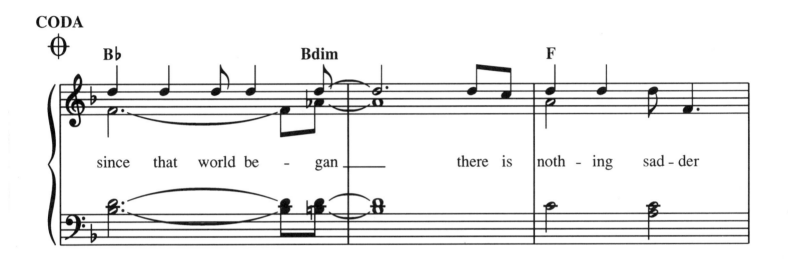

since   that   world be - gan _____   there is   noth - ing   sad - der

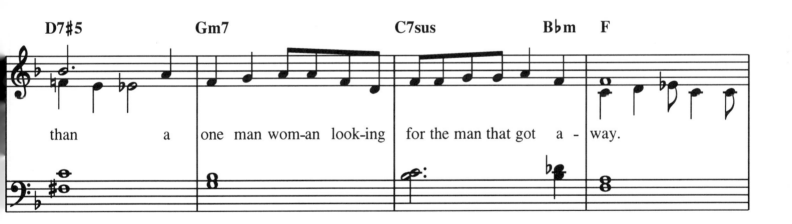

than   a   one man wom-an look-ing for the man that got a - way.

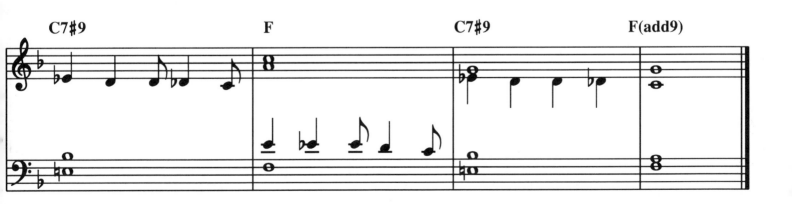

MISTY

Words by JOHNNY BURKE
Music by ERROLL GARNER

65

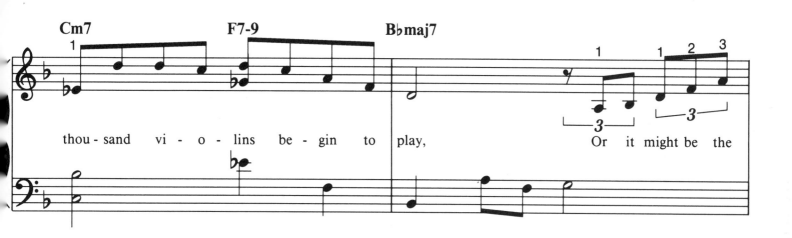

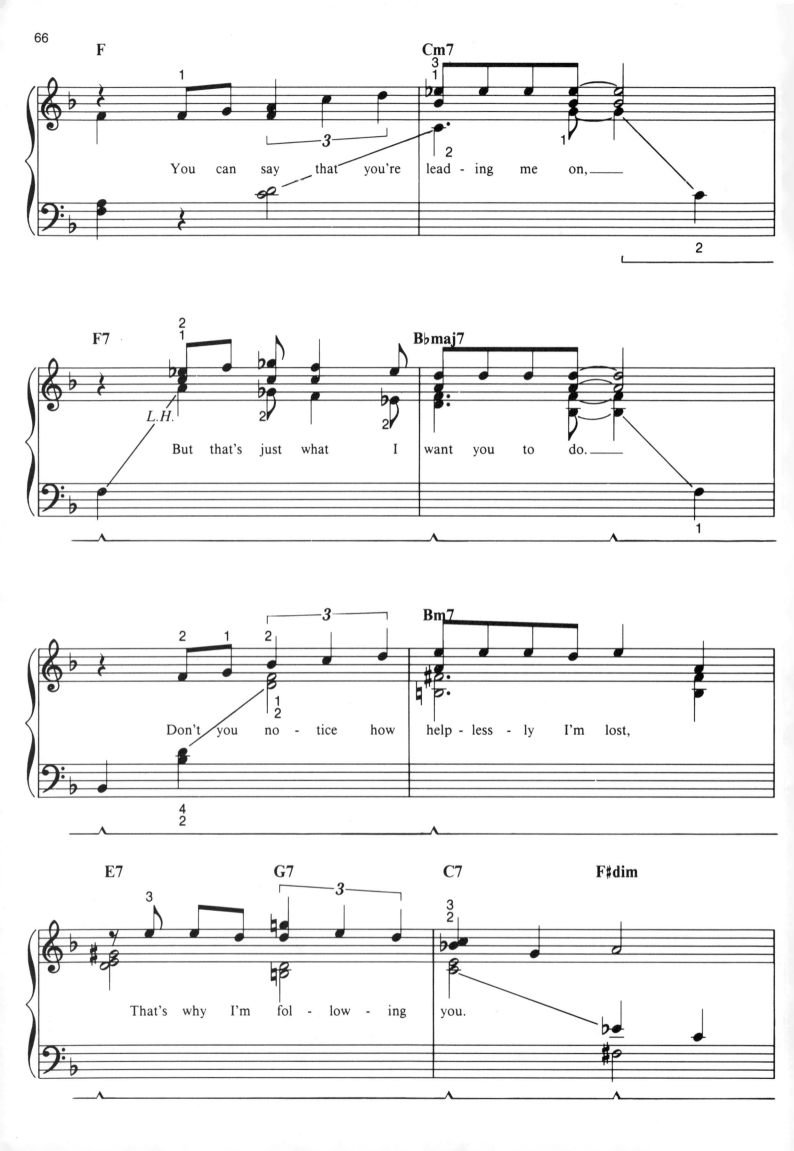

66

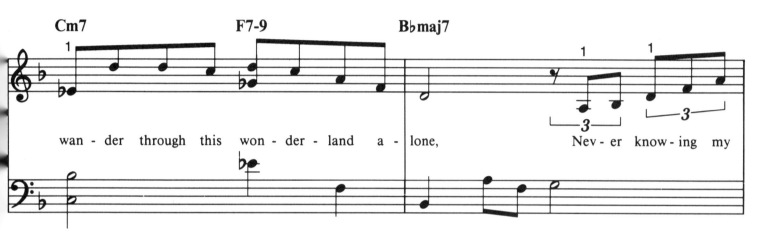

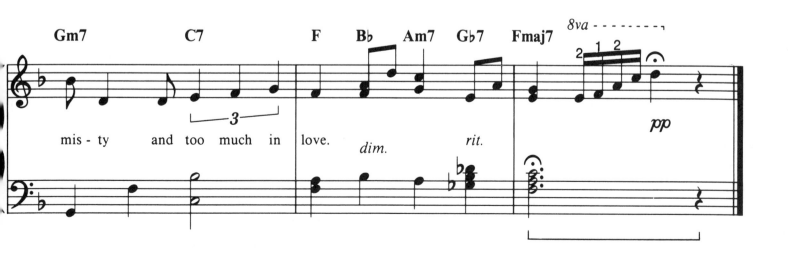

MORE THAN YOU KNOW

Words by WILLIAM ROSE and EDWARD ELISCU
Music by VINCENT YOUMANS

69

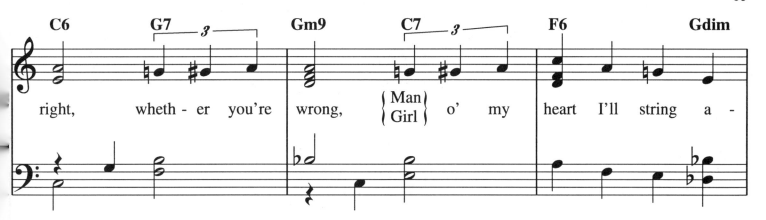

right, wheth - er you're wrong, {Man/Girl} o' my heart I'll string a -

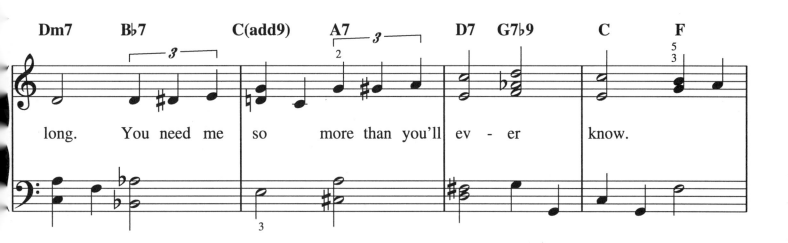

long. You need me so more than you'll ev - er know.

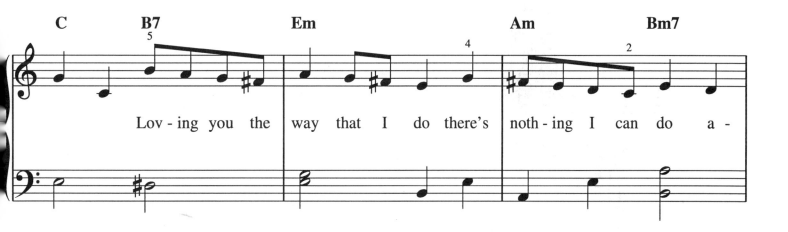

Lov - ing you the way that I do there's noth - ing I can do a -

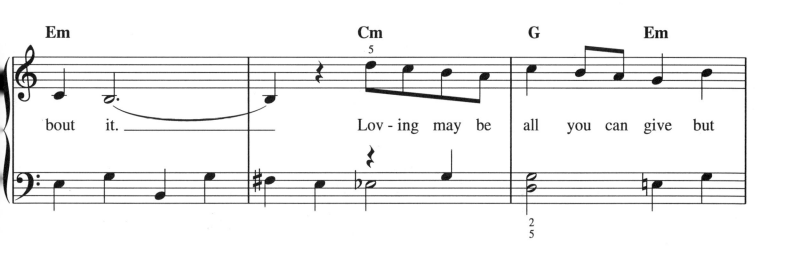

bout it. _____ Lov - ing may be all you can give but

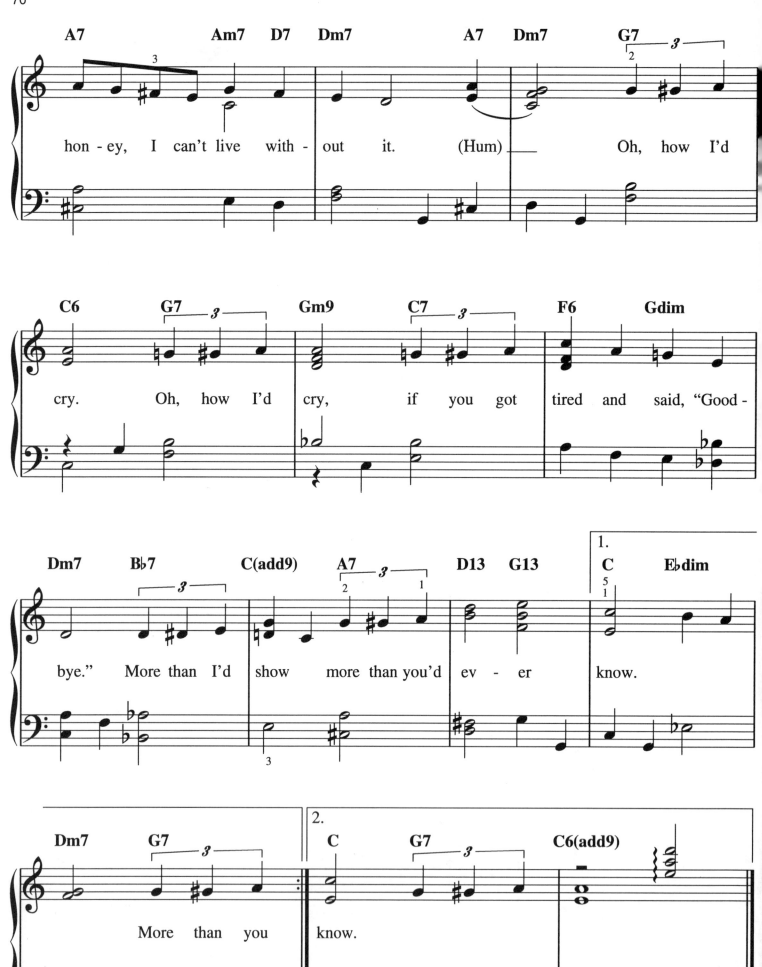

MY FOOLISH HEART
from MY FOOLISH HEART

Words by NED WASHINGTON
Music by VICTOR YOUNG

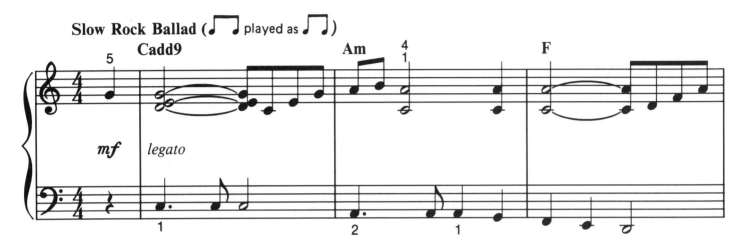

72

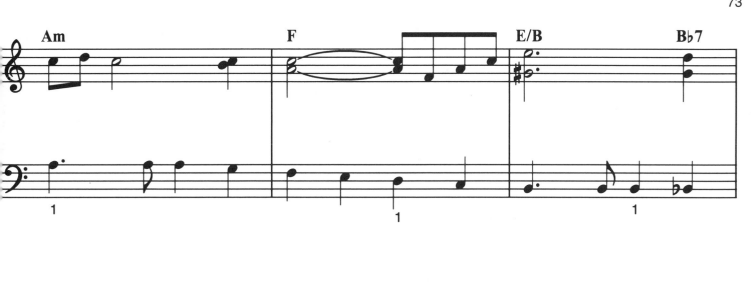

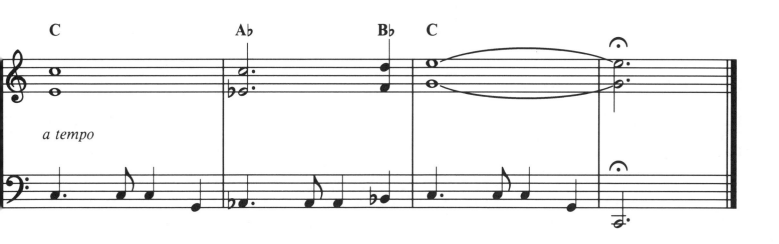

MY FUNNY VALENTINE

from BABES IN ARMS

Words by LORENZ HART
Music by RICHARD RODGERS

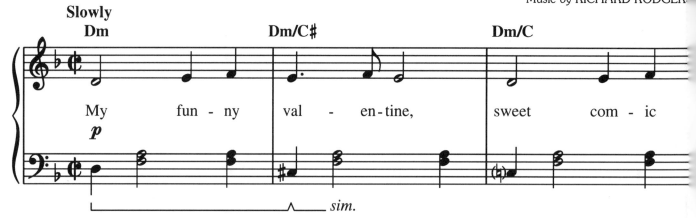

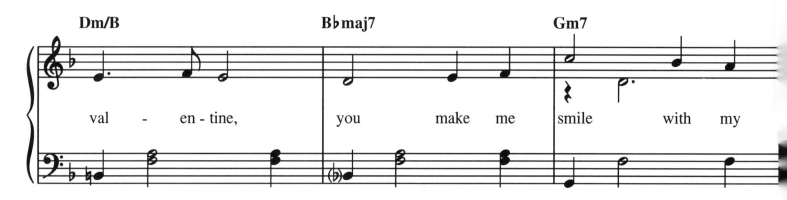

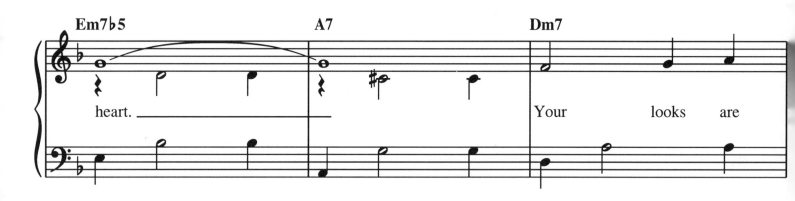

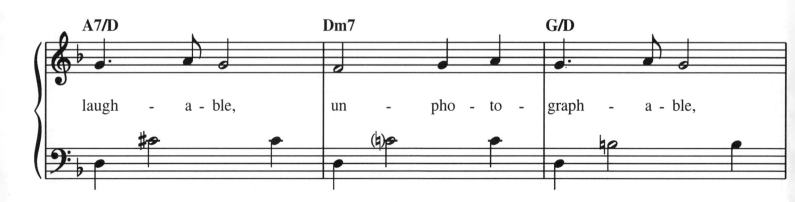

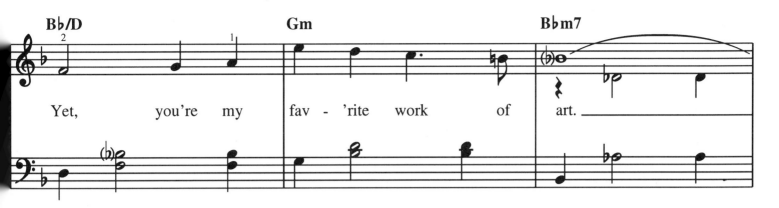

Yet, you're my fav - 'rite work of art. ____

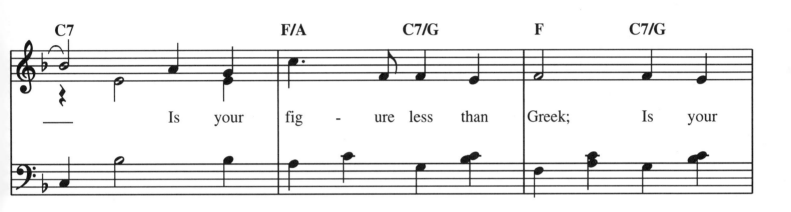

____ Is your fig - ure less than Greek; Is your

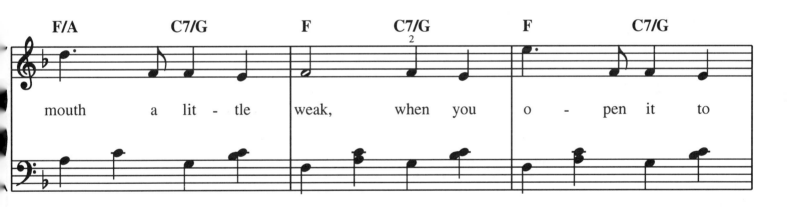

mouth a lit - tle weak, when you o - pen it to

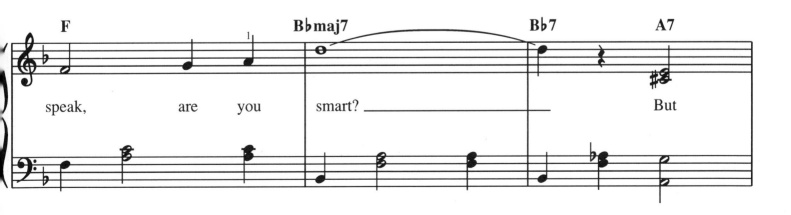

speak, are you smart? _____ But

76

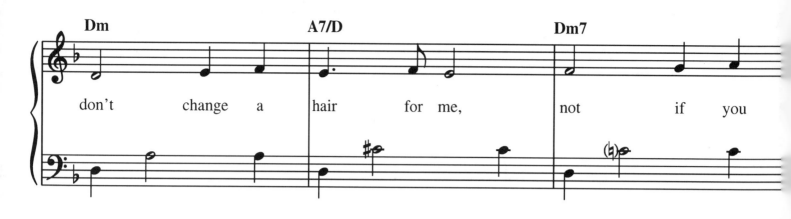

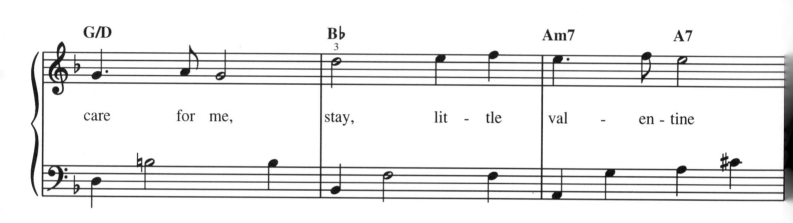

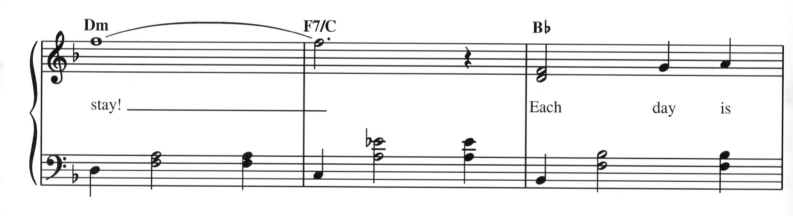

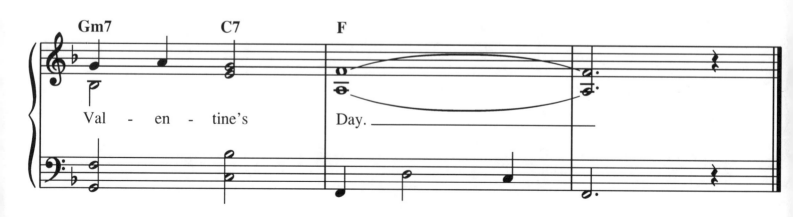

NOBODY'S HEART

from BY JUPITER

Words by LORENZ HART
Music by RICHARD RODGERS

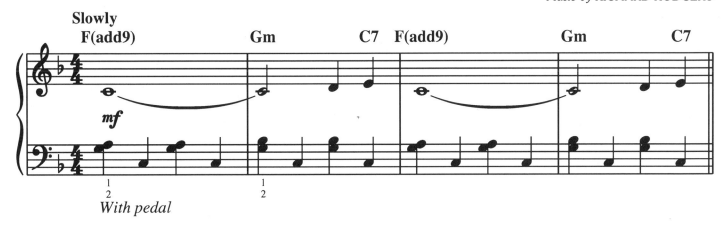

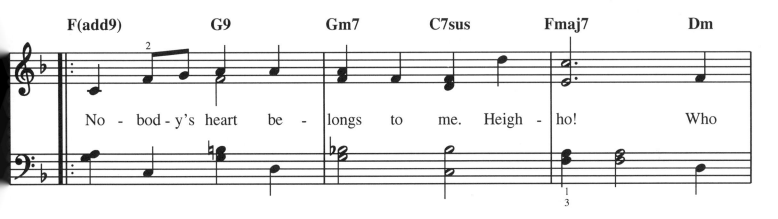

No - bod - y's heart be - longs to me. Heigh - ho! Who

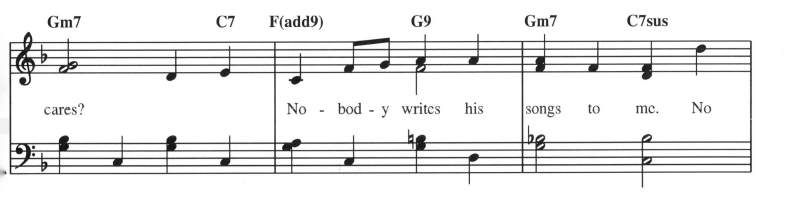

cares? No - bod - y writes his songs to me. No

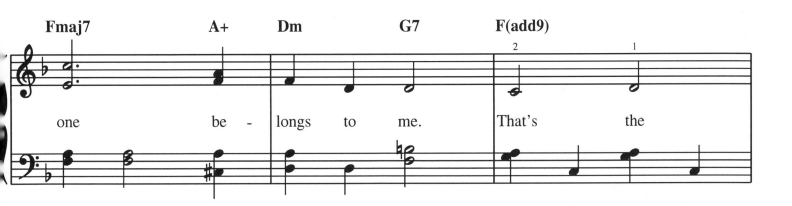

one be - longs to me. That's the

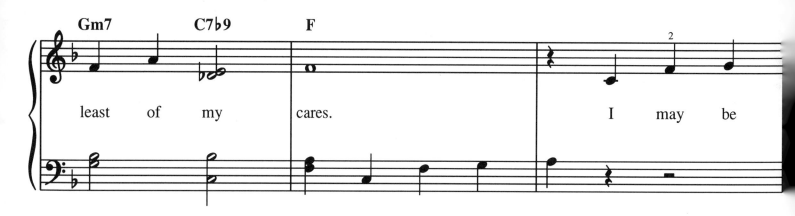

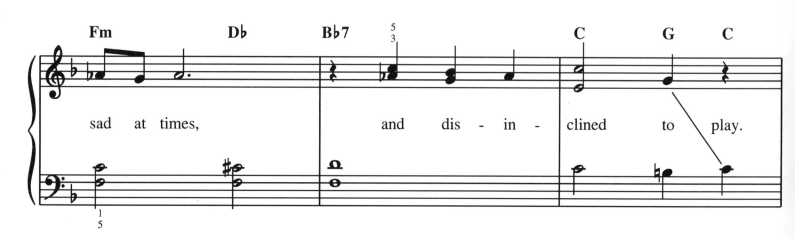

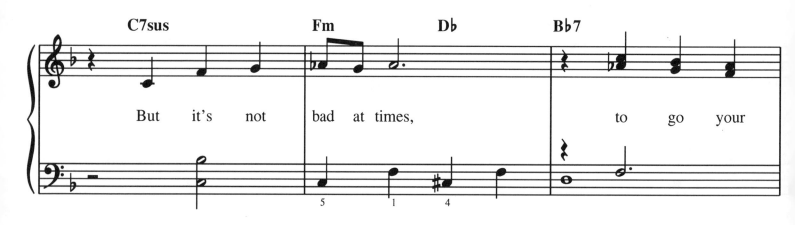

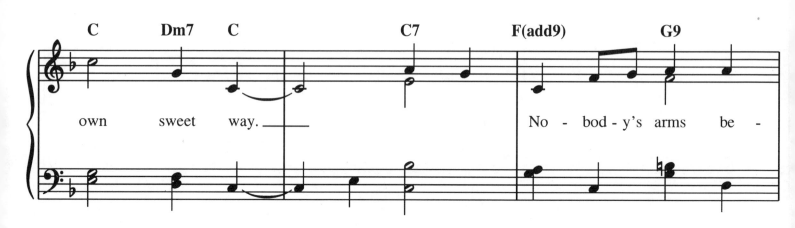

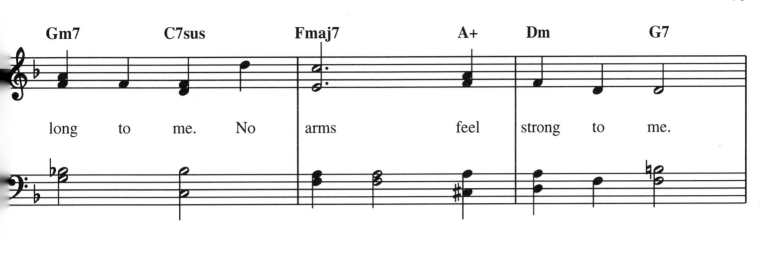

long to me. No arms feel strong to me.

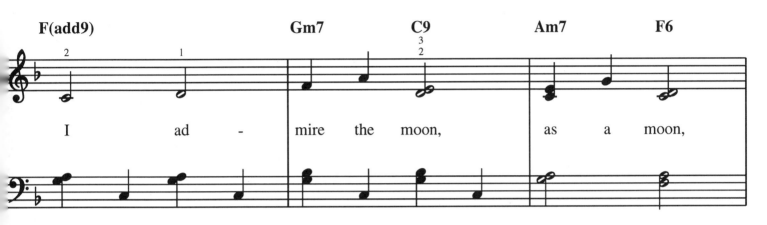

I ad - mire the moon, as a moon,

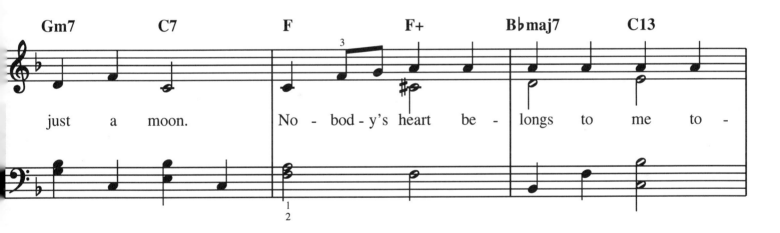

just a moon. No - bod - y's heart be - longs to me to -

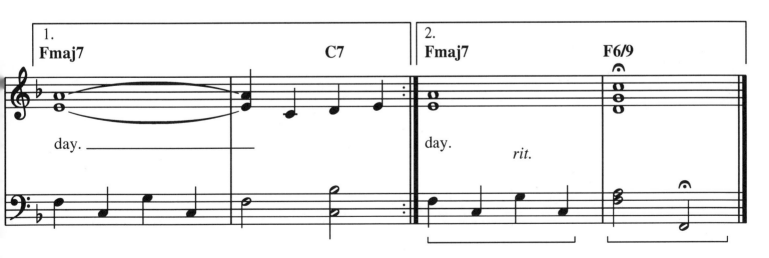

1.
day. _____

2.
day. *rit.*

ONE FOR MY BABY

(And One More for the Road)

from the Motion Picture THE SKY'S THE LIMIT

Lyric by JOHNNY MERCER
Music by HAROLD ARLEN

It's quar-ter to three, there's no one in the place ex - cept you and me. So, set 'em up, Joe. I've got a lit - tle sto - ry

got the rou - tine, so drop an - oth - er nick - el in the ma - chine. I'm feel - in' so bad I wish you'd make the mu - sic

that's how it goes, and Joe, I know you're get - ting anx-ious to close. So, thanks for the cheer, I hope you did - n't mind my

you ought - a know.
dream - y and sad.
bend - ing your ear.

We're drink-ing, my friend,
Could tell you a lot,
This torch that I've found

B♭ **B♭9** **F**

to the end ____ of a brief ep - i - sode.
but you've got ____ to be true to your code.
must be drowned _ or it soon might ex-plode.

Make it

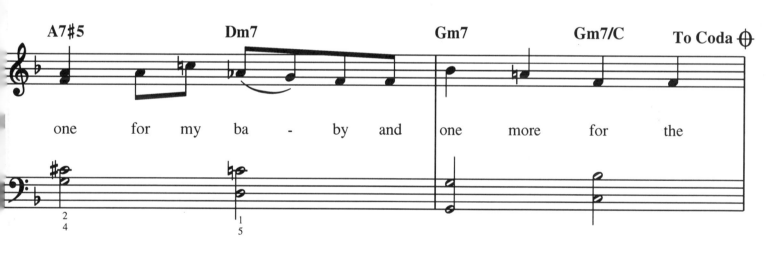

A7♯5 **Dm7** **Gm7** **Gm7/C** **To Coda** ⊕

one for my ba - by and one more for the

1.
F **Gm7** **C7**

road. I

2.
F **Cm7** **F9**

road. You'd

never know it, but bud-dy, I'm a kind of po-et, and I've

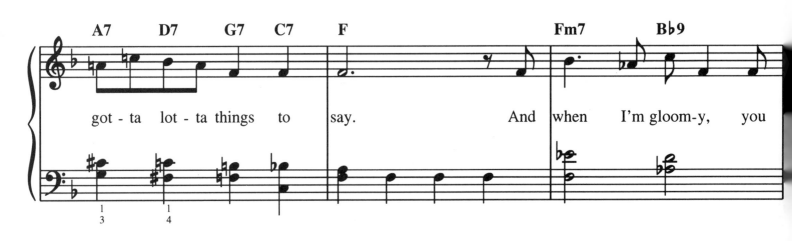

got-ta lot-ta things to say. And when I'm gloom-y, you

sim-ply got-ta lis-ten to me, un-til it's talked a-way. Well,

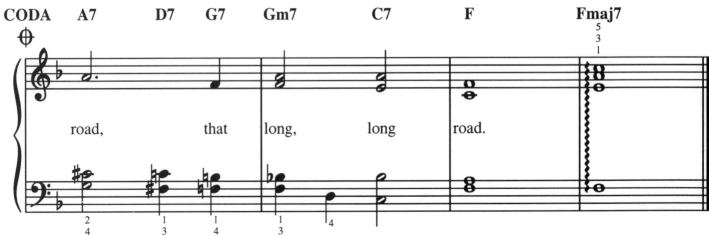

road, that long, long road.

THE PARTY'S OVER
from BELLS ARE RINGING

Words by BETTY COMDEN and ADOLPH GREEN
Music by JULE STYNE

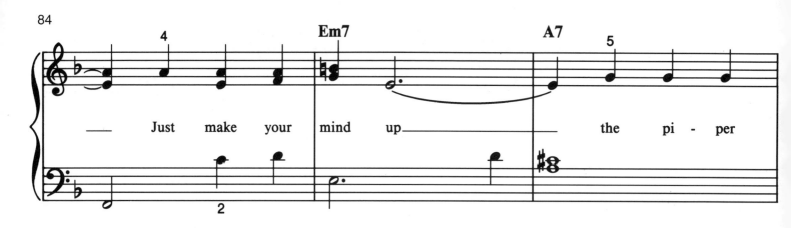

Just make your mind up___ the pi - per

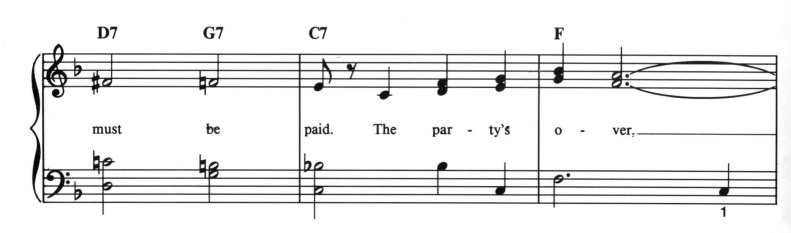

must be paid. The par - ty's o - ver,___

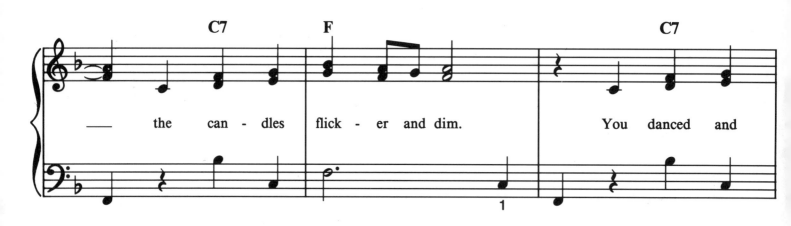

___ the can - dles flick - er and dim. You danced and

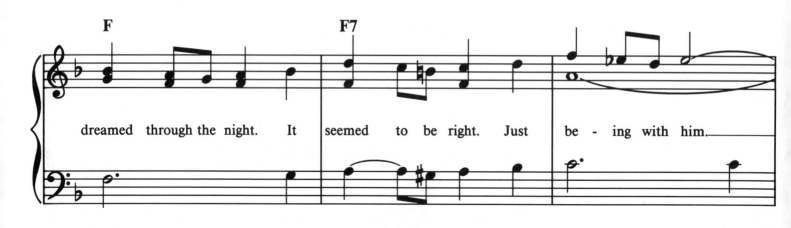

dreamed through the night. It seemed to be right. Just be - ing with him.___

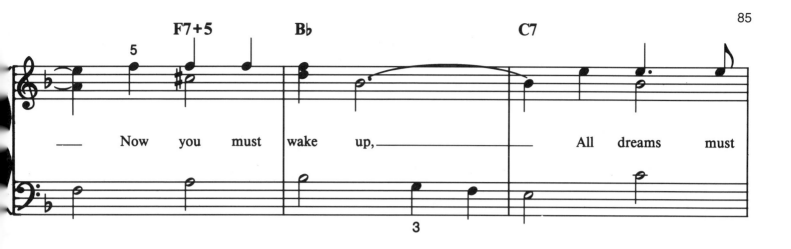

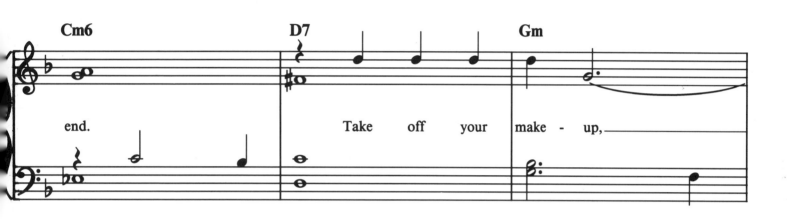

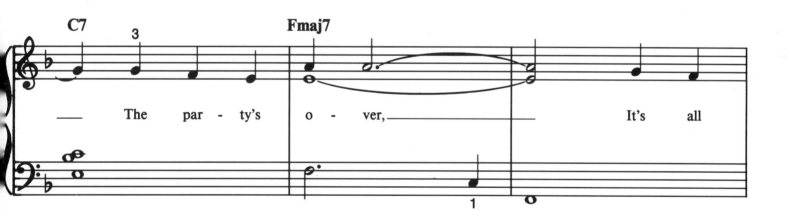

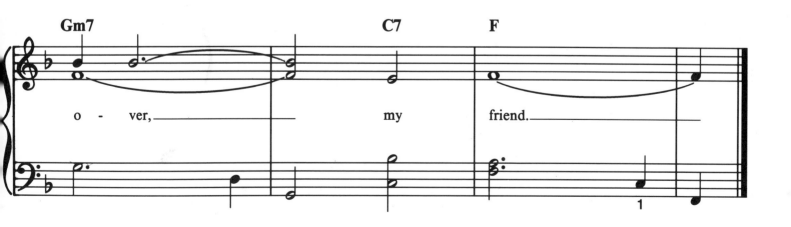

SO IN LOVE

from KISS ME, KATE

Words and Music by
COLE PORTER

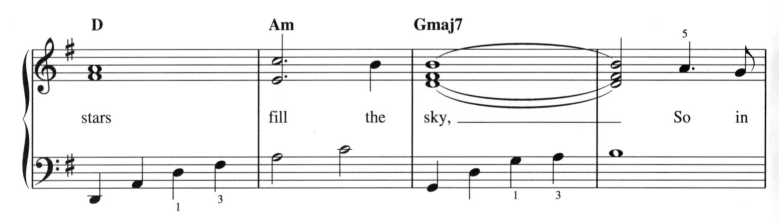

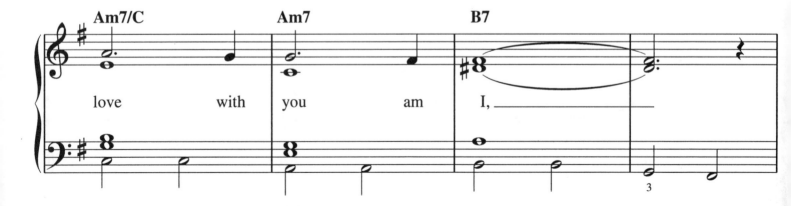

87

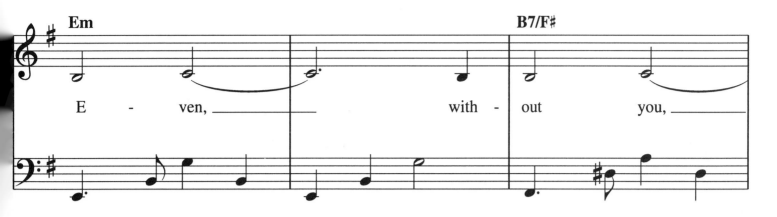

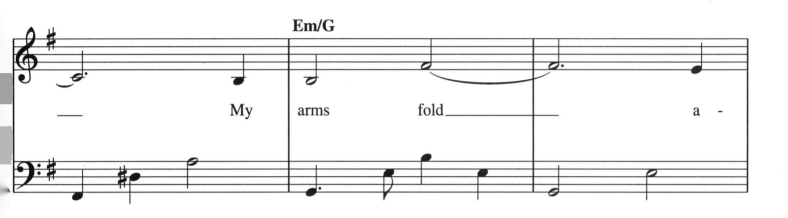

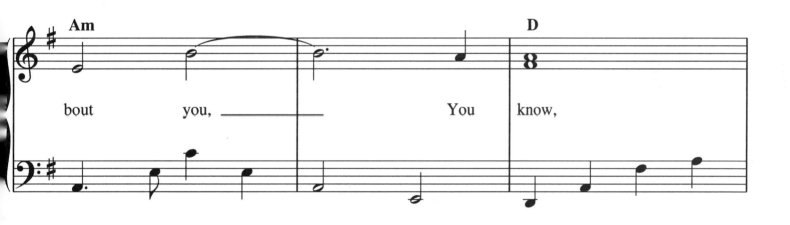

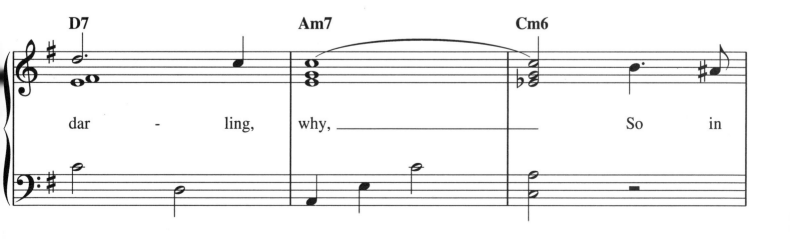

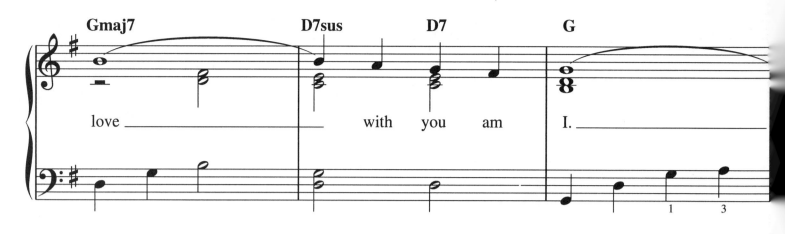

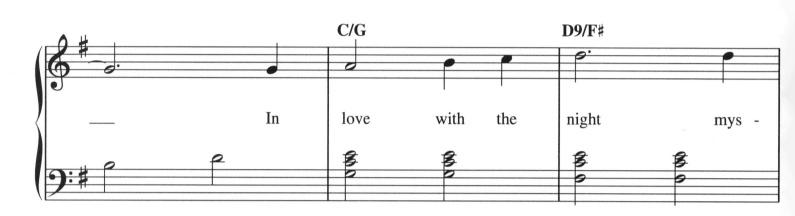

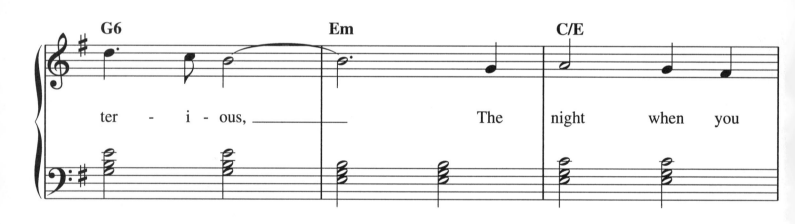

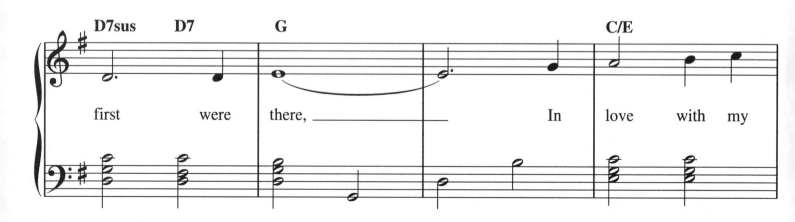

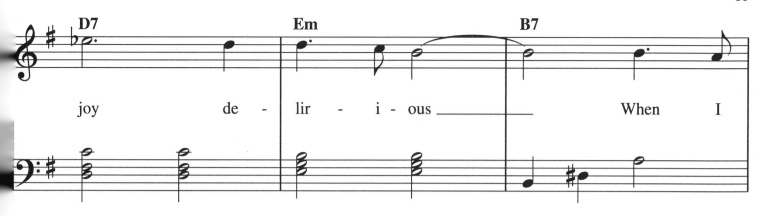

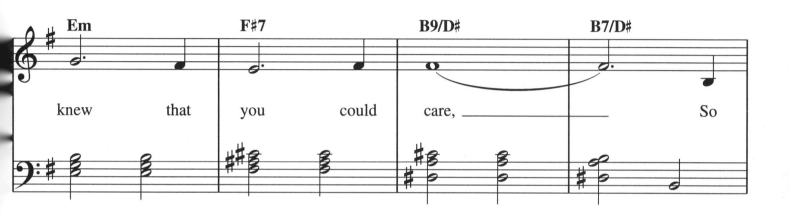

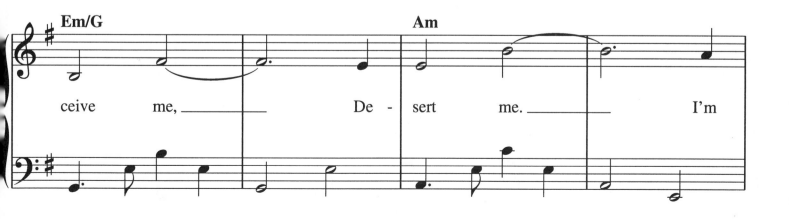

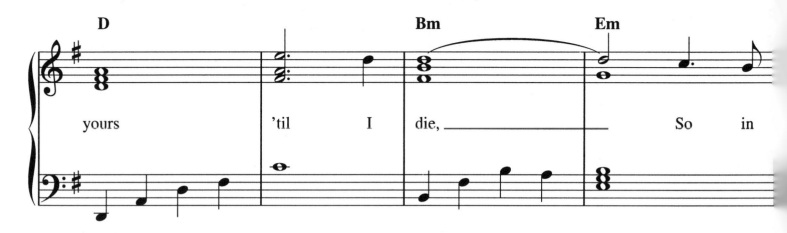

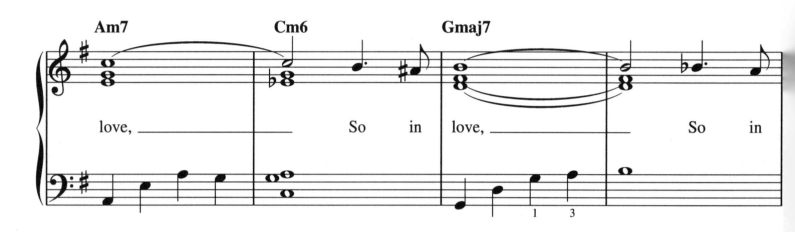

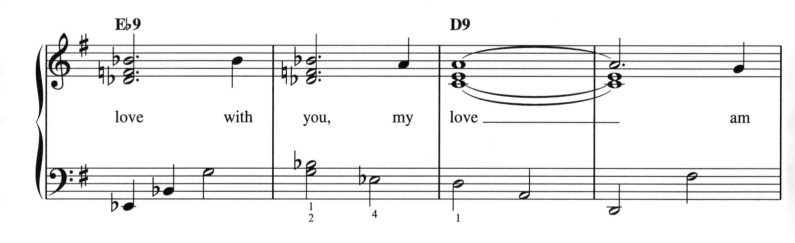

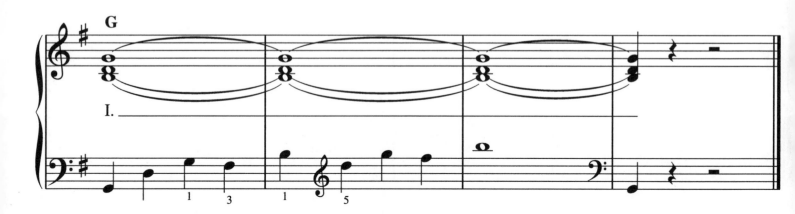

STORMY WEATHER
(Keeps Rainin' All the Time)
from COTTON CLUB PARADE OF 1933
featured in the Motion Picture STORMY WEATHER

Lyric by TED KOEHLER
Music by HAROLD ARLEN

92

TEN CENTS A DANCE

from SIMPLE SIMON

Words by LORENZ HART
Music by RICHARD RODGERS

Slowly with a jazz feel

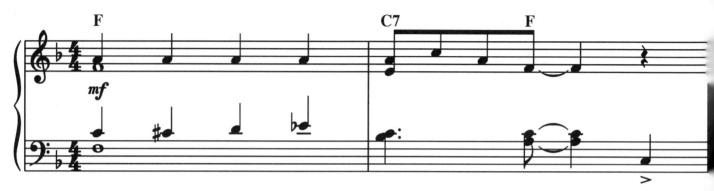

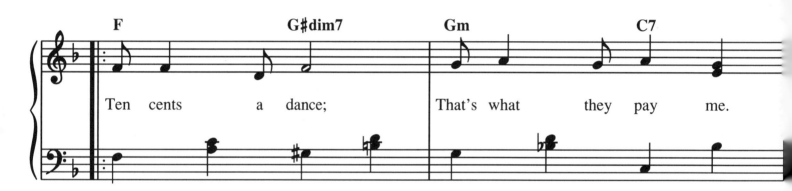

Ten cents a dance; That's what they pay me.

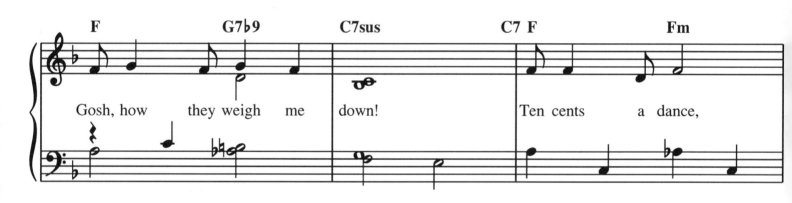

Gosh, how they weigh me down! Ten cents a dance,

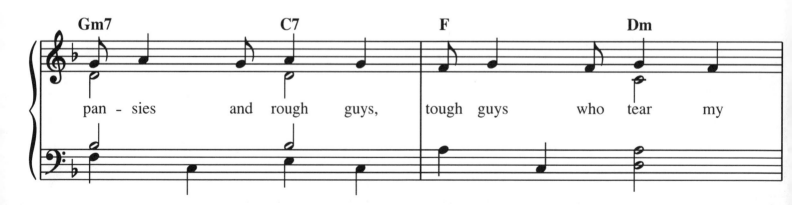

pan - sies and rough guys, tough guys who tear my

gown! Sev - en to mid - night I hear drums,

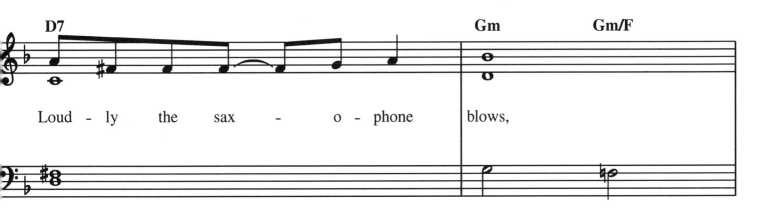

Loud - ly the sax - o - phone blows,

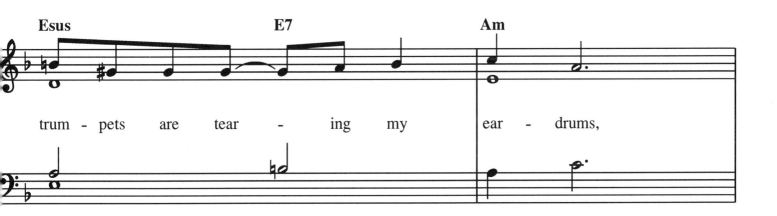

trum - pets are tear - ing my ear - drums,

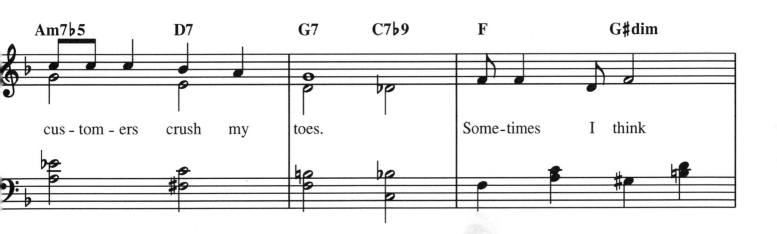

cus - tom - ers crush my toes. Some-times I think

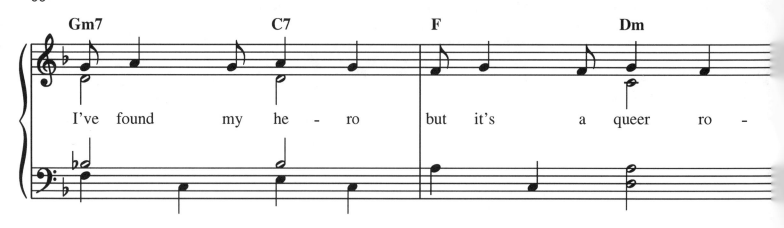

I've found my he - ro but it's a queer ro -

mance. All that you need ___ is a

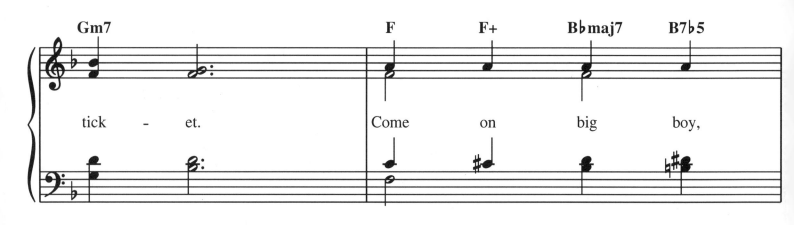

tick - et. Come on big boy,

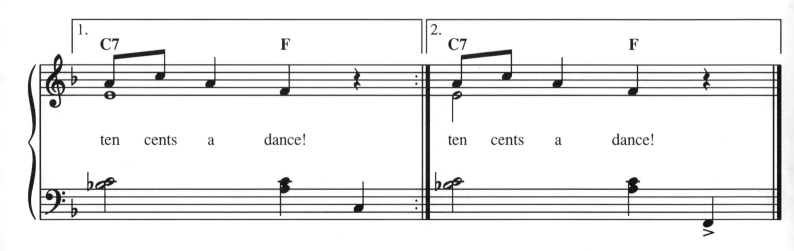

1. ten cents a dance!

2. ten cents a dance!

WHY WAS I BORN?

from SWEET ADELINE

Lyrics by OSCAR HAMMERSTEIN II
Music by JEROME KERN

Slowly (in 2)

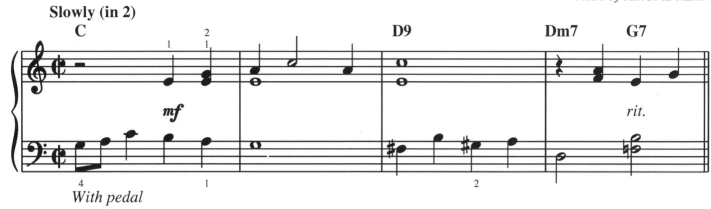

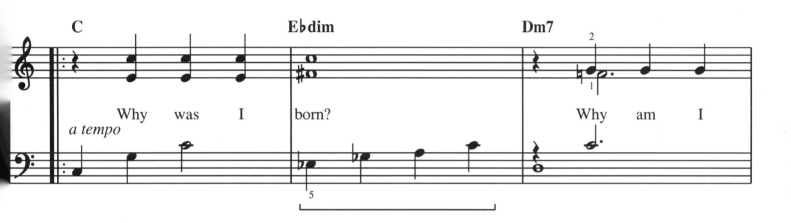

Why was I born? Why am I

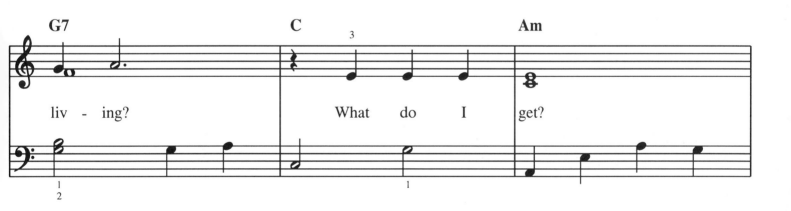

liv-ing? What do I get?

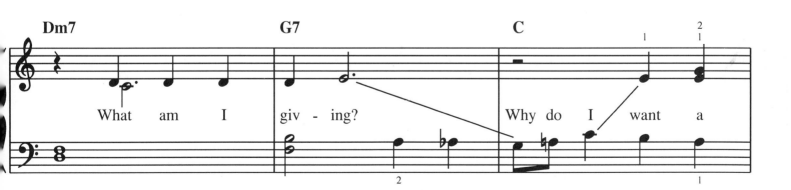

What am I giv-ing? Why do I want a

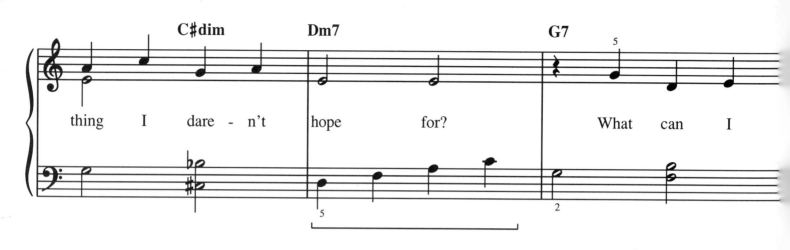

C#dim Dm7 G7

thing I dare - n't hope for? What can I

Gm7 C7 F Em7 Am7

hope for? _____ I wish I knew.

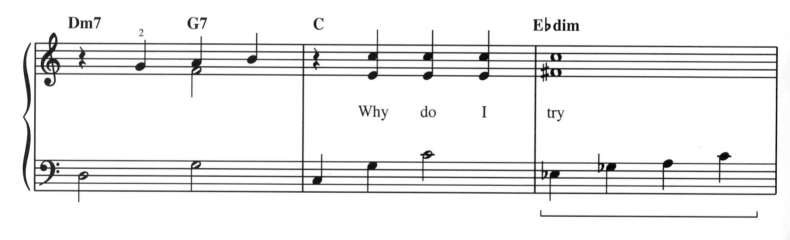

Dm7 G7 C E♭dim

Why do I try

Dm7 G7 C

to draw you near me? Why do I

WHY DON'T YOU DO RIGHT

(Get Me Some Money, Too!)

By JOE McCOY

102

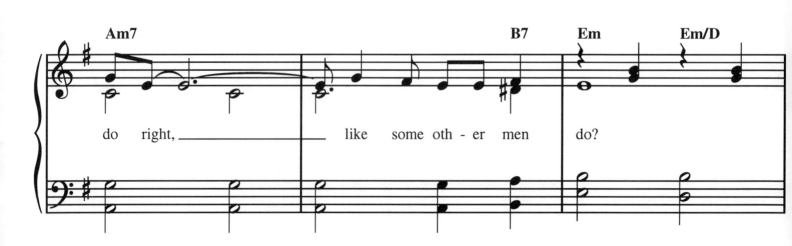

It's Easy To Play Your Favorite Songs with Hal Leonard Easy Piano Books

The Best of Today's Movie Hits
16 contemporary film favorites: Change The World • Colors Of The Wind • I Believe In You And Me • I Finally Found Someone • If I Had Words • Mission: Impossible Theme • When I Fall In Love • You Must Love Me • more.
00310248 ....$9.95

Rock N Roll For Easy Piano
40 rock favorites for the piano, including: All Shook Up • At The Hop • Chantilly Lace • Great Balls Of Fire • Lady Madonna • The Shoop Shoop Song (It's In His Kiss) • The Twist • Wooly Bully • and more.
00222544..$12.95

Playing The Blues
Over 30 great blues tunes arranged for easy piano: Baby, Won't You Please Come Home • Chicago Blues • Fine And Mellow • Heartbreak Hotel • Pinetop's Blues • St. Louis Blues • The Thrill Is Gone • more.
00310102..$12.95

I'll Be Seeing You
50 Songs Of World War II
A salute to the music and memories of WWII, including a chronology of events on the homefront, dozens of photos, and 50 radio favorites of the GIs and their families back home. Includes: Boogie Woogie Bugle Boy • Don't Sit Under The Apple Tree (With Anyone Else But Me) • I Don't Want ... Moonlight In Vermont

......................$17.95

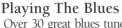

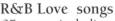

The Best Songs Ever
A prestigious collection ... songs, featuring: All I Ask ... Beast • Body And S... Crazy • Don't Kno... Me To The Moon • ... Here's That Rainy Day • Imagine • In The Mood • Let It Be • Longer • Moonlight In Vermont • People • Satin Doll • Save The Best For Last • Somewhere Out There • Stormy Weather • Strangers In The Night • Tears In Heaven • What A Wonderful World • When I Fall In Love • and more
00359223 ....$19.95

...Hunchback Of ...ctions
...Disney's animated classic, complete with beautiful color illustrations. Includes: The Bells Of Notre Dame • God Help The Outcasts • Out There • Someday • and more.
00316011..$14.95

Country Love Songs
34 classic and contemporary country favorites, including: The Dance • A Few Good Things Remain • Forever And Ever Amen • I Never Knew Love • Love Can Build A Bridge • Love Without End, Amen • She Believes In Me • She Is His Only Need • Where've You Been • and more.
00110030 ....$12.95

Today's Love Songs
31 contemporary favorites, including: All I Ask Of You • Because I Love You • Don't Know Much • Endless Love • Forever And Ever, Amen • Here And Now • I'll Be Loving You Forever • Lost In Your Eyes • Love Without End, Amen • Rhythm Of My Heart • Unchained Melody • Vision Of Love • and more.
00222541...$14.95

R&B Love songs
27 songs, including: Ain't Nothing Like The Real Thing • Easy • Exhale (Shoop Shoop) • The First Time Ever I Saw Your Face • Here And Now • I'm Your Baby Tonight • My Girl • Never Can Say Goodbye • Ooo Baby Baby • Save The Best For Last • Someday • Still • and more.
00310181 Easy Piano......................$12.95

Best Of Cole Porter
Over 30 songs, including: Be A Clown • Begin The Beguine • Easy To Love • From This Moment On • In The Still Of The Night • Night And Day • So In Love • Too Darn Hot • You Do Something To Me • You'd Be So Nice To Come Home To • and more
00311576..$14.95